FAMILY CONNECTIONS

Other products from Northwest Media Inc., developed with Dr. Patricia Chamberlain:

Focus on Minding — a 30-minute video with Viewer's Manual

Foster and Adoptive Care situations with children, Ages 6-12 — a 15-minute video with Leader's Guide

Foster Care Solutions: Learning to Problem Solve — a two-part video with Viewer's Manual

For a copy of our current catalog of all foster care resources, including our Independent Living series, please call Northwest Media Inc. or visit our web site at:

http://www.northwestmedia.com

A Social Interactional Approach

VOLUME 5

FAMILY CONNECTIONS

A Treatment Foster Care Model
for Adolescents with Delinquency

Patricia Chamberlain, Ph.D.

Oregon Social Learning Center
Eugene, Oregon

326 West 12th Avenue
Eugene, Oregon 97401
800-777-6636 • 541-343-6636

Copyright © 1998
by Northwest Media Inc.
10 9 8 7 6 5 4 3 2 1

All rights reserved. No part of the book may be reproduced by any means, nor transmitted, nor translated into a machine language with the written permission of the publisher. Excerpts may be printed in connection with published reviews without permission.

ISBN 1-892194-00-7

Printed in the United States of America
Copies of this book may be ordered from the publisher

Editorial and Production Credits
Editor-in-Chief: Scot Patterson
Copy Editor: Virginia Rich
Interior Design and Page Composition: Guy Kudlemyer
Cover Concept: Scot Patterson, Guy Kudlemyer, and Patricia Chamberlain
Cover Design and Illustration: copyright © 1994 by Lightbourne Images

Dedication

To the Antoine family: Karla, Bob, Tara, Katie, Nick, and Pat — they were the first to put *treatment* in our Treatment Foster Care program. And to the other devoted families who followed.

Contents

Foreword	x
About the Author	xii
Acknowledgments	xiii
Preface	xv
Introduction	1
Characteristics of Antisocial Children	2
Planning a Treatment Strategy	3
Building on the TFC Model	3
Treatment Rationale	4
Our Mission	6
Chapter 1	
Characteristics of Monitor Program Participants	9
Case Study: Phil's Wild Ride	9
From Conduct Problems to Later Delinquency	11
A Four-Stage Developmental Model	12
Characteristics of Monitor Program Youths	14
Monitor Program Goals	15
Summary	16
Chapter 2	
Recruitment, Screening, and Preservice Training of Treatment Foster Parents	17
Characteristics of Successful Foster Parents	17
Recruitment and Screening	19
Preservice Training Course	21
Guidelines for Working with Foster Parents	24
Summary	25
Chapter 3	
Preparing the Adolescent and Foster Parents for the Placement	27
Preparing the Adolescent for Placement	27
Getting the Foster Parents Ready for the Placement	28
The Level System	29
Overview of the Three-Level System	30
Level System Charts	33
Point System Economy	37
Case Example: Brian and the Bet	40
Summary	43

Chapter 4
Family Treatment for the Child's Biological or Adoptive Parents — 45
- Establishing a Working Relationship — 45
- Setting Up the Placement — 49
- Weekly Family Therapy Sessions — 50
- Case Example: John Learns to Talk to His Mother — 54
- Actions and Reactions — 55
- Summary — 55

Chapter 5
Individual Therapy for the Child — 57
- The Acceptance Meeting — 57
- The Initial Phase of Treatment — 58
- The Reenactment Technique — 61
- Teaching Social and Relational Skills — 63
- Case Example: The Boy with the Incredible Brain — 64
- Summary — 65

Chapter 6
Case Management One: Working with Foster Parents, Biological Parents, and Therapists — 67
- Case Example: Jay's Pipe Dream — 71
- Summary — 72

Chapter 7
Case Management Two: Coordinating Services with Other Community Agencies — 73
- School Liaison — 73
- Parole or Probation Staff Liaison — 76
- Case Example: Jimmy Decides to Skip School — 76
- Liaison with Judges — 77
- Summary — 78

Chapter 8
Aftercare Services for Children and Families — 79
- Reducing the Risks Associated with Transitions — 79
- Teaching and Supporting Families in Aftercare — 80
- Case Example: Lee Learns an Important Lesson — 83
- Respite Care — 83
- Customizing Aftercare Services — 84
- Summary — 84

Chapter 9
Outcome Evaluation of Treatment Foster Care Program Participants   85
Study 1: Effectiveness of TFC for Delinquent Youth   *85*
Study 2: TFC for Emotionally Disturbed Youths   *89*
Summary   *95*

Chapter 10
Methods of Case and Program Evaluation   97
The Parent Daily Report Checklist   *97*
Clinical Applications of PDR in TFC Programs   *100*
Summary   *103*

Appendixes   105

Appendix 1
Introduction for Foster Parents: Program Values, Policies, and Procedures   *107*

Appendix 2
Agreement Between the Foster Parents and the Program   *113*

Appendix 3
Parental and Youth Consent Forms for Participation in the Program   *125*

Appendix 4
Program Overview   *127*

References   129

Author Index   139

Foreword

It took twenty-two offenses, eight arrests, four social workers, two court counselors, a family therapist, and a judge before one troubled youth was referred to the Monitor Program at OSLC. It was clear that this was destined to be a new adventure, one that would possibly lead to a dramatic change in the self-destructive trajectory of this adolescent's life course.

There is an African saying that is gaining acceptance in both the popular and professional press: "It takes an entire village to raise one child." We need to embrace this notion in our culture as well. Ideally, every child should be protected, nurtured, socialized, and mentored by his or her immediate family. In turn, the immediate family should be protected and supported by the extended family, neighbors, and the community. In our idealized village, the child would be universally regarded as having extraordinary value to the community at large. This would provide a protective cocoon in which to raise and socialize the child. If the child behaved badly down the street, adults in the neighborhood would provide corrective feedback; if the mother or father became ill or incapacitated, the grandparents would fill in or even move in.

Our modern society has become more complex and dangerous, which means that children need the protection and socialization that only can be provided by a strong and caring family. The concept of family as it is used here doesn't necessarily have anything to do with biology — it is a perpetual-motion loving, teaching, and protecting machine. Unfortunately, at precisely the time in history when the institution of the family is most critical, it has lapsed into metamorphosis. Although the end point of the rapid changes taking place is not clear, it has become apparent that many children no longer have a safe developmental cocoon. Young families are being torn apart by social and economic stressors.

Although systemic interventions could be used to help the majority of struggling families intensify the mentoring, monitoring, discipline, and encouragement that is so crucial to successful childrearing, more and more families are disintegrating to the point that social agencies must recommend or mandate out-of-home placements. Fortunately, foster care families are able to provide for the critical developmental needs of children whose own families are no longer able to help them. Traditionally, the primary function of foster families has been to offer security and affection to children in temporary need, but such families also can provide a structured environment and specialized therapy for children who are seriously at risk for psychological, behavioral, and educational adjustment problems.

On the basis of over two decades of work in developing parent training technologies for difficult and high-risk children at clinical research centers such as the Oregon Social Learning Center, Dr. Chamberlain has taken the next step in developing a program model that gives children from dysfunctional homes a second chance. Treatment Foster Care provides the intensive and comprehensive family support that *every* child needs to have a successful childhood and adolescence. Dr. Chamberlain has developed a unique and highly successful strategy for selecting, training, and supporting treatment foster families. The Monitor Program has been consistently evaluated and improved over the last ten years. It provides special needs children with normative socialization experiences and behavioral and educational support, and at the same time helps the child's family of origin pull itself together and develop the skills they need to raise their children.

I have done a lot of work in the areas of family intervention, parent training, and the prevention of conduct problems in children. I have also consulted with Dr. Chamberlain and her colleagues since the mid-1980s. This is a *nice* program.

John B. Reid *July, 1994*

About the Author

Patricia Chamberlain, Ph.D., founded the OSLC Treatment Foster Care program model in 1983. She has continued to direct TFC programs and conduct research on the model for the past 14 years. She is a board member and chair of the research committee of the Foster Family-Based Treatment Association, an international group of agencies conducting TFC programs. Dr. Chamberlain regularly serves on grant application review committees for the National Institute of Mental Health. She is the author and co-author of numerous journal articles and book chapters on treatment process, outcome research, methodology, parental use of discipline, and on foster care and related topics. Dr. Chamberlain is currently Clinical Director of the Oregon Social Learning Center in Eugene, Oregon.

Acknowledgments

The program model described here is the result of a collaborative effort that began in the early 1970s and continues today. Many colleagues at the Oregon Social Learning Center have been instrumental in the development of this approach. They include John Reid, J. P. Davis, Marion Forgatch, Karla Antione, Gerald Patterson, Kate Kavanagh, Alison Prescott, Kevin Moore, Kathy Reid, and Lew Bank. Gerry Bouwman and Judy Boler have been supportive and innovative in dealing with administrative issues. Irma August at the Genesis School in Portland, Oregon, and Keith Flicker and Malcom Tabor from the Oregon State Children's Services Division were instrumental in getting the program off the ground. Jake Terpstra from the Children's Bureau and Jim Breiling from the National Institute of Mental Health have helped in the conceptualization and implementation of research on our TFC programs. Bob VanIderstein, our juvenile probation officer; Diane Poynter from Children's Services Division; and Judges Edwin Allen and James Hargraves have provided us with a strong local support base. Special thanks to Scot Patterson, the editor, for his careful and thoughtful work on this book.

Funding for our TFC programs has come from a variety of sources. The Monitor Program has been funded by the state Children's Services Division since November 1983. Funds for conducting research on that program have come from the National Institute of Mental Health, Violence and Traumatic Stress Branch, and from the Department of Education, Office of Special Education Programs, Division of Innovation and Development. The TFC program for severely emotionally disturbed youngsters was originally funded by a grant from the Department of Health and Human Services, Children's Bureau, and has subsequently been funded by a collaboration between the local Children's Services Division office and Title XIX Medicaid funds. Funding for developing and studying the aftercare treatment component has been provided by the Department of Health and Human Services, Children's Bureau.

As we attempt to fit the needs of the children whom we serve into "allowable program expense" categories, we encounter gaps that often do not require large sums of money to bridge but that are extremely important to the child or family. For instance, basic frames for glasses are a covered medical expense, but designer frames or contact lenses are not. For some teenagers, this fact determines whether or not they will have their vision corrected, because they simply refuse to wear glasses that make them "look stupid." Gifts from the Catherine M. and Edwin W. Davis Foundation through Mr. and Mrs. Fredrick W. Davis have made it possible for us to respond to this kind of need, provide for individualized academic assistance, and offer support for activities such as hobbies and sports.

During our years of service, we have been fortunate to work with a number of outstanding and dedicated foster parents. These individuals and their families have routinely extended themselves beyond their job descriptions to provide care, support, assistance, extra time, and their own financial resources to help the youngsters placed with them. Being a foster parent for teenagers with severe and long-standing problems is a demanding and often thankless job. The bad press the foster care system receives makes one wonder why any family would subject itself to being a foster care provider. Our success in recruiting and maintaining the services of excellent foster parents is the foundation of our TFC programs. We are extremely grateful to these families, who continually show that they are willing to confront and embrace the needs of the children placed in their care.

Preface

This book provides a detailed description of the Treatment Foster Care programs that began at the Oregon Social Learning Center (OSLC) in 1983. The primary focus is on the Monitor Program that was developed for youths who were referred from or who were at-risk for placement in state training schools. A similar treatment program for adolescents with severe emotional disturbance also is discussed, but to a lesser extent, throughout the book. The outcome studies that have been completed at OSLC indicate that the Treatment Foster Care model is an effective vehicle for helping these clinical populations, which have been difficult to treat with other approaches. This book reviews the programs developed at OSLC and provides guidelines for implementing similar programs in other settings. The title *Family Connections* was selected because the foster care model described here capitalizes on the tremendous positive potential of families. Both the foster families whom we hire to be key therapeutic agents and the biological or adoptive families of the adolescents are the central focus of this book.

Chapter 1 reviews the characteristics of the youths who have participated in our Treatment Foster Care programs. Studies on the progression from early conduct problems to later delinquency are also discussed. The "nuts and bolts" of recruitment, screening, and preservice training of foster parents are presented in Chapter 2. Chapter 3 covers the development and implementation of a daily behavior management system in the foster home. Chapters 4 and 5 describe the individual therapy provided to the adolescents and the family therapy for their parents or relatives. Chapters 6 and 7 review the system used for case management, including methods for ongoing supervision and training of the foster parents, coordination with project therapists, and liaison with the schools and juvenile courts. A program for providing follow-up services once the adolescent has returned home is outlined in Chapter 8. Chapter 9 summarizes the data from the treatment evaluation studies that have been conducted on the Monitor Program and a similar program developed for children with severe emotional disturbance. Chapter 10 reviews the assessment methods used to evaluate case and program progress, the Parent Daily Report checklist, and gender differences in responding to the Monitor Program.

The reader should be aware of several conventions that have been used throughout this book. In the professional literature and in practice, the model is interchangeably called "Treatment Foster Care" and "Specialized Foster Care." In this book it is called the Treatment Foster Care model because that label seems more descriptive. The national professional organization representing such programs calls itself the Foster Family–Based Treatment Association. Another convention adopted in this book is the use of the pronoun he to describe participants in the program, when he or she would have been more appropriate. Although 75% of the youths who have participated in the program are males, the model also applies to females with similar problems (see discussion in Chapter 10).

Requests for information about the two foster care programs developed at OSLC have increased steadily as the programs have become more established and the findings from preliminary studies have been published. Our model also has received more attention as our focus has expanded to include children and adolescents with a variety of presenting problems. Professionals from the fields of social work, criminal justice, psychology, and psychiatry are beginning to consider Treatment Foster Care as a viable alternative to group treatment approaches. This book is intended to provide practical information on the day-to-day workings of our TFC programs as well as a discussion of related clinical and theoretical issues.

To remain relevant and vital, community programs must continue to change and adapt. This process is ongoing within our TFC programs. The purpose of this book is not to describe a program model that has arrived at some level of perfection but to present a way of thinking about designing and implementing interventions for youths with serious and long-standing problems that require them to be placed outside their family homes. The guiding principle in our TFC programs is to prepare the child and his family for the child's eventual return home. Our commitment to this goal provides a sense of direction as we continue to develop and refine the treatment methods outlined in this volume.

INTRODUCTION

The Treatment Foster Care (TFC) model has its roots in both the foster care system and the deinstitutionalization movement of the 1960s and 1970s. During the 1980s and early 1990s, the number of TFC programs has greatly increased (Hudson, Nutter, & Galaway 1990). In addition, the focus of established TFC programs has become more diversified to address the needs of children, adolescents, and families with a wide range of serious problems (e.g., Dennis 1992). The TFC model appeals to both clinicians and policy makers because it is cost-effective, it places the child in the least restrictive setting possible, and it minimizes the influence of peers with similar problems. In recent years, many group homes have been converted to the TFC model. Hudson, Nutter, and Galaway (1990) conducted a survey of more than 400 established TFC programs throughout the United States and Canada. They found that most of these (51%) had been developed since 1985; this included both new programs and those converting from group residential care to TFC. In that survey, the authors also reported on the types of agencies developing TFC programs and the types of referrals that they received. Seventy percent of the programs surveyed were administered by nonprofit agencies. The programs received approximately 10% of their referrals from the juvenile justice system and 75% from the child welfare system; approximately one-half of the children in the latter group were under the age of 12. Although it is not known whether the programs surveyed are representative of TFC programs in the United States, it is clear that the number and types of TFC programs in the United States and Canada are rapidly expanding.

In his 1983 book *Special Foster Care,* Brad Bryant reviews the history of the development of the model, its key components, and the advantages of TFC over institutional and group care. Although he advocates expansion of the model, he concludes that it is imperative to develop practical training methods as the first step toward that goal. In addition, he asserts that training should be conducted by persons who have direct experience using the model.

Despite the rapid expansion of TFC programs, few empirically-based studies have been conducted that have evaluated the effectiveness of the approach. This fact is not surprising, given the difficulty of conducting well-controlled research in community settings (Boruch 1987) and the reluctance of the state agencies that usually fund TFC programs to dedicate resources to evaluation. A few noteworthy exceptions include the work by Hawkins, Meadowcroft, Almeida, Fabry, and their colleagues at the Pressley Ridge Schools in Pittsburgh (Hawkins et al. 1992; Hawkins, Almeida, & Samet 1989; Hawkins et al. 1985; Martin & Hawkins 1992). The book edited by Hawkins and Breiling (1989) reviews a variety of critical issues, including the origins of the TFC model, implementation of TFC in different contexts, training and supervision, and evaluation methods.

The advantages of the TFC model have been discussed by Bryant (1980) and others

(Galaway et al. 1990). It has been used with diverse target populations, including children with special needs (such as emotional or conduct problems), and children with serious and chronic illnesses or who are medically fragile (see Yost, Hochstadt, & Charles 1988). The general TFC program model allows for considerable flexibility in the specific population treated and the intervention used. The model capitalizes on the ability of carefully selected and trained foster families to implement a treatment plan. Because TFC focuses on treating the *individual* by placing each child in a different family setting, it is possible for a given program to provide placements for a heterogenous population of children and adolescents. Another advantage is that the development and implementation of the child's treatment plan are not limited by considerations of group fairness or group goals as they are in residential group care.

The Monitor Program developed in 1983 at the Oregon Social Learning Center (OSLC) is based on the TFC model. To date, the program has served more than 150 adolescents. The youths who have participated in the Monitor Program were adolescents with a history of chronic delinquency who were at-risk for placement in, or discharged from, state training schools. In 1986, the original Monitor Program was modified to address the clinical needs of 80 additional children and adolescents who were referred from the Oregon State Hospital or the local Children's Services Division branch office because they were judged to be severely emotionally disturbed. Although the Monitor Program is the main focus of this book, the treatment outcome data for both populations are reviewed in Chapter 9. The sections that follow establish a context for examining the components of the Monitor Program by reviewing the issues relating to the development and implementation of interventions for youths with conduct problems and antisocial behavior.

CHARACTERISTICS OF ANTISOCIAL CHILDREN

It is a formidable challenge to devise effective treatments for adolescents with established patterns of antisocial behavior. The prognosis for their long-term adjustment is bleak; they are at-risk for a variety of problems in adulthood, including criminality, erratic employment, dependence on welfare systems, accidents, alcoholism, and poor relationships (Robins 1966). Several well-conducted retrospective and prospective longitudinal studies have provided convincing evidence that most forms of antisocial behavior have their roots in early childhood (e.g., Elder, Caspi, & Downey 1983). Once established, early antisocial patterns tend to follow a predictable developmental course that gradually leads to more extreme problem behaviors.

By the time antisocial children begin attending school, they often have inadequate social skills, academic problems in the classroom, and difficulty getting along with their peers on the playground. Early experiences in the antisocial child's home have typically laid the groundwork for a high rate of noncompliance and an abrasive style of interacting with others. The child has "learned" to use high-amplitude coercive strategies to maximize short-term gains. Over time, this leads to rejection by parents, peers, and teachers. The antisocial child misses out on many of the normal opportunities for socialization. Gerald Patterson uses the term *deviancy drift* to describe the rejection process experienced by antisocial children; as they approach adolescence, these children seek out deviant peers, activities, and values.

Studies on peer relationships have shown

that rejected children tend to associate with one another, even though when asked they report that they would prefer to associate with their more popular peers. Children who are rejected by their peers usually do not participate in mainstream activities such as sports or Boy Scouts. During adolescence, many of these youths report that they have strong affiliations with peers who engage in antisocial behavior. It has been found that children who associate with deviant peers are at risk for chronic delinquency as adolescents (Elliott, Huizinga, & Ageton 1985).

PLANNING A TREATMENT STRATEGY

Reversing this rejection process involves planning and implementing a coordinated set of interventions that, for each case, target the child's behaviors and his relationships with parents, peers, and teachers. The strategy of simultaneously "attacking all fronts" was developed as the result of a series of clinical trials conducted at OSLC since the early 1960s with families of antisocial children. Of particular relevance is a study conducted by Patterson and Reid (Bank et al. 1991) in which an intervention was designed for a group of chronic delinquent adolescents and their parents. To participate in the study, the adolescents had to have a record of at least three previous offenses (only one of which could be nonstatus). The intervention involved having the parents and teenagers attend separate weekly therapy sessions. During these sessions, the therapist worked with the parents to improve their family management skills and helped them learn to communicate and negotiate more effectively with their adolescents. Therapy with the teenagers focused on developing skills in areas such as resisting peer pressure, problem solving, and appropriate school behavior.

After treating only a few cases, we realized that we had encountered a major obstacle. Because the families were continually immersed in crises, it was difficult to help the parents change less urgent issues such as how they disciplined and supervised their problem teenagers. We spent most of our time putting out the fires that remained after the crises had passed. It became apparent that the only way we could work on making changes would be to slow down the torrent of problems that were impinging on the family. Unfortunately, many of these crises were generated by the target adolescent. These teenagers had severe conduct disorders, which meant they were having problems in multiple settings: at school, in the community, and at home with their siblings and parents. Consequently, a treatment model that focused on improving the parents' family management skills and providing skill training for the teenager was not powerful enough. The effectiveness of the treatment also was compromised by the fact that we had little control over the teenager's unsupervised time or peer relations, both of which had been shown in numerous studies to be strong predictors of delinquency.

BUILDING ON THE TFC MODEL

It was against this backdrop that in 1983 we applied for state funding to develop a Treatment Foster Care (TFC) program model based on the social learning treatment approach. Conduct-problem teenagers who had been removed from their homes because of delinquency were placed, one per family, with specially selected and trained parents in the community. The foster parents were selected on the basis of their parenting skills, and they received both initial and ongoing training in effective techniques for managing an antisocial, aggressive adolescent. During the placement, the teenager's biological parents also attended therapy sessions; now that a major source of stress had been removed (the program teenager), the parents were in a better position to make changes in their family as well. The program included working in coordination with school personnel and carefully monitoring the adolescent's peer relationships. We called it the "Monitor Program."

The objective of the Monitor Program was to change the negative trajectory of antisocial behavior for delinquent teenagers by improving their social adjustment with their family members and peer group. This required designing interventions for both the home and school settings and carefully supervising the youths throughout their day. The treatment model described here builds on previous research and clinical work conducted at OSLC (e.g., Patterson et al. 1975; Patterson, Chamberlain, & Reid 1982) and elsewhere (e.g., Forehand & Long 1991; Webster-Stratton & Hammond 1990). The model emphasizes the importance of using significant adults, such as parents and teachers, to act as agents of change or interventionists for the child. To be effective, these adults must be trained to react systematically to the child's problem and prosocial behaviors. Therapeutic reactions have the following characteristics: they are consistent, contingent, and generally supportive. Appropriate targets for the intervention include decreasing covert and overt forms of antisocial behavior, increasing the child's appropriate behavior, and building prosocial skills.

TREATMENT RATIONALE

It is generally accepted that environmental factors such as parenting practices make a significant contribution to the development and later stability of antisocial behavior in children. Recent work has highlighted the role of specific parenting practices, such as poor supervision and ineffective discipline strategies, as prime determinants of subsequent delinquency (Patterson, Reid, & Dishion 1992; McCord 1979).

In a reanalysis of data from longitudinal studies, Loeber and Dishion (1983) found that composite measures of parental family-management practices were the best predictors of later delinquency. This was true even when these composite measures were compared with other variables that also had good predictive value, such as previous ratings of children's behavior problems, criminality of other family members, poor academic achievement, separation from parents, and socioeconomic status. Laub and Sampson (1988) reported that for a matched sample of 500 delinquents and nondelinquents, parenting practices mediated 80% of the effects of socioeconomic variables such as household overcrowding and economic dependence, as well as the father's criminality and drunkenness. Patterson's longitudinal analyses have emphasized specific parenting practices as predictors of delinquency. In a study of 206 boys from high-risk neighborhoods, Patterson and his colleagues found that the parents' level of success at supervising and disciplining their fourth-grade children accounted for significant variance in predicting which children would become delinquent three to six years later (Patterson, Reid, & Dishion 1992). These studies support the premise that specific day-to-day parenting practices, such as style of supervision and discipline, are key mechanisms that mediate the effects of other background or structural variables often correlated with delinquency.

Interventions designed to change parenting practices as a way of impacting child conduct problems have been developed and studied since the advent of the behavioral parent training movement in the early 1960s. Numerous treatment outcome studies have focused on changing the parents' and teacher's day-to-day interactions with and reactions to the conduct-problem child. Many of these studies indicate that the child's aggressive, antisocial behavior patterns can be altered by teaching parents to systematically attend to their child's behavior, reinforce positive behaviors, and provide contingent, consistent discipline for negative child behaviors (Taplin & Reid 1977; Miller & Prinz 1990; Patterson, Chamberlain, & Reid 1982; Webster-Stratton, Kolpacoff, & Hollingsworth 1988). Effective discipline methods used in the context of a supportive environment provide corrective experiences that teach the antisocial child cooperation and compliance skills. In his book *Treatment of Antisocial Behavior in Children and Adolescents*, Kazdin (1985) concluded that parent-training interventions are a promising approach for the treatment of child conduct problems.

Several studies have documented the relationship between inconsistent discipline and child conduct problems (Zucker 1976; Rutter, Shaffer, & Sturge 1975; Patterson 1976b). Exposure to poor discipline practices not only puts the child at-risk for developing conduct problems but also contributes to maintaining and escalating the severity of these problems once they have become established. McCord, McCord, and Zola (1959) found that parental inconsistency was a good predictor of the continuation of child conduct problems. The review of recent correlational studies of mother–child interaction by Wahler and Sansbury (1990) showed that maternal inconsistency is a maintenance factor for child oppositional problems.

Many investigators have speculated about the specific processes that result from inconsistent parental discipline. Wahler and Dumas (1986) assert that parents who are inconsistent in their use of discipline inadvertently "prime" their child's oppositional or aggressive behavior. The studies reviewed in Patterson (1982) show that inconsistent parents get caught in a "reinforcement trap" whereby short-term gains such as cessation of the child's coercive behavior actually strengthen the child's difficult behavior over the long term. Two processes come into play: The parent's lack of follow-through directly reinforces the child's negative or coercive behaviors, and the child's subsequent coercive behaviors become increasingly resistant to extinction. These processes have received empirical support in several studies (Sawin & Parke 1979; Gardner 1988).

In addition, it has been shown that irritable or explosive parental discipline is related to child aggression (Sears, Maccoby, & Levin 1957; Hetherington & Martin 1979), hyperactivity (Stevens-Long 1973), and antisocial and delinquent behavior (Farrington 1978; Gleuck & Gleuck 1968; Pulkkinen 1983). Characteristics such as depression, antisocial patterns, social isolation, and stress increase the likelihood that adults will engage in patterns of chronically irritable or explosive discipline (Rutter & Quinton 1984; Kochanska 1991; Gelfand & Teti 1990).

Several well-documented longitudinal studies have demonstrated a strong relationship between poor parental supervision and delinquency. For example, Wilson (1987) found that for a sample of boys from high-crime areas, 80% of the families who had shown lax supervision when their children were 10 to 11 years old had one or more delinquent sons; the comparable figure for families with strict supervision was 30%. Farrington (1978) found that 8-year-old children who experienced poor parental supervision and harsh discipline practices were at significantly greater risk for aggression and violence in adolescence. In their reanalysis of the Gleucks' data, Laub and

Sampson (1988) found that poor maternal supervision in conjunction with discipline characterized by the use of threats and physical punishment were the most important predictors of serious and persistent delinquency.

From these studies, it may be concluded that poor supervision and ineffective discipline are the parenting practices most strongly related to children's aggression and delinquency. How well parents supervise their children seems to provide a general indication of parental functioning. Good supervision implies that the family is well organized, and it may also suggest that the parents have the ability to use effective discipline methods. For parents to be good supervisors, they must be involved in the child's day-to-day activities to the extent that they have accurate information regarding where the child is and who he or she is associating with. Parents who do a good job of supervising their children are more likely to have clearly stated house rules and expectations, and they are more consistent about following through when their children break rules. When children are carefully supervised and receive encouragement from their parents for engaging in prosocial activities, it reduces the influence of a deviant peer group. In addition, close monitoring of the child's behavior at school and completion of homework is essential for helping the child improve his or her academic performance. Academic failure has been found in several studies to relate to depressed mood (Kellam 1990; Weinberg & Rehmet 1983) and poor peer relations (Patterson & Capaldi 1991).

Undoubtedly, some children and teenagers are more difficult for parents to deal with than others. Empirically, it is equally plausible that the relation between discipline and supervision and child problems could be explained by child characteristics and behaviors as by poor parenting practices. Adolescents with serious problems are more defiant during discipline confrontations and offer more resistance to supervision than their nonproblem peers. A high level of parenting skill is required to provide severely disturbed or delinquent youths with corrective experiences. Parents also need a good support network to deal with an adolescent's daily outbursts of aggression or antisocial behavior. Even the most skilled and committed adult is likely to become irritable and experience a sense of failure at times when working with a difficult youngster; therefore, it is important to give treatment foster parents ongoing support and consultation while they are working with conduct-problem teenagers.

OUR MISSION

Ultimately, the success of our program depends on our ability to recruit, select, train, supervise, and support talented foster parents who are willing to devote themselves to implementing a daily treatment program for chronically delinquent or disturbed children and teenagers. The goal of the program is to systematically change the child's social environment to control antisocial behavior and encourage appropriate prosocial behavior and development of academic skills. Typically, to minimize the influence of deviant peers, only one child is placed in each TFC home.

A daily treatment plan is developed for each child and is implemented in the foster home. Close supervision and consistent, contingent, nonviolent discipline methods are emphasized in the daily treatment plan. This plan is augmented by individual therapy for the child, family therapy for the child's parent(s), and a corresponding program that is set up with the child's school and parole or probation officer. The typical TFC placement lasts six months. The family therapy sessions focus on improving the supervision, discipline, and encouragement skills of the child's biological parents, relatives, or other aftercare resources. Frequent visits home, conducted throughout the placement, provide opportunities for parents and their children to practice the "nuts and bolts" of their individualized program. This sets the stage for the teenager's eventual return home. Our goal is to initiate and coordinate changes in the adolescent (and sometimes in his or her siblings) and to teach the parents how to set reasonable limits and provide good supervision so the child returns to a home environment that will support his prosocial development.

CHARACTERISTICS OF MONITOR PROGRAM PARTICIPANTS

This chapter describes the characteristics of the teenagers who have participated in the Monitor Program. Typically, they were referred by juvenile court workers or a judge because of problems with chronic delinquency. The average number of arrests prior to intake for the cumulative sample of Monitor Program youths to date is 10.84 for boys (S.D. = 5.87) and 8.43 for girls (S.D. = 4.12). In each case, it was determined by the court that the adolescent needed an out-of-home placement, and he or she was referred to the Monitor Program in lieu of commitment to one of the two state training schools in Oregon. The Monitor Program was originally funded in 1983 by the State of Oregon, Children's Services Division, as one of 11 statewide "Community Alternatives to Institutionalization Programs." Of the more than 150 youths who have participated so far, three-fourths were placed in the Monitor Program to "divert" them from state training schools, and one-fourth had already spent some time there prior to being referred to our program.

Before reviewing the summary data on the characteristics of these adolescents, a brief case study is provided to give readers a sense of how a typical case might present at intake.

CASE STUDY: PHIL'S WILD RIDE

Phil was 14 years old when he was referred to the Monitor Program. He had a record of six prior arrests: two for burglary, two for the unauthorized use of a motor vehicle, and two for criminal mischief. The referral problems were listed as follows: "family issues, lack of supervision and parenting skills, alcohol probably still a problem at home, stepfather has not been involved in any treatment, Phil is failing at school and has poor attendance." The list of family strengths included the attachment between Phil and his mother. Although Phil's mother did not want to have him placed outside the home, she was resigned that "something had to happen."

The Last Straw

Phil's problem behavior was becoming more serious — the latest charges against him involved stealing three cars and some related damages. In the first car theft, Phil was accompanied by a friend. The two boys took a pickup truck and drove it into town. At that point, Phil's friend apparently decided that he did not want to be involved anymore and arranged to have his parents pick him up at a convenience store. Phil continued driving the pickup until he came to the parking lot of a car repair business. When he saw the keys in the ignition of a truck parked there, he left the pickup he had been driving and took the other truck, which had a standard shift. He backed into the street successfully, but stalled the truck so that it was perpendicular across the street. He abandoned the truck in the street and got into a Thunderbird, which also had the keys in the ignition. He then backed the Thunderbird out of the parking lot and ran into the stalled truck! The police had arrived by that time, and Phil was arrested and taken to juvenile detention. During the course of this incident, Phil caused over $10,000 in damage. Because Phil had a previous record of multiple arrests and had failed to comply with an intensive probation program, the court ordered placement in residential care.

Referral Information

A psychological evaluation showed that Phil met the DSM-III-R diagnostic criteria for Conduct Disorder (classification 312.20), and provisionally met the criteria for Developmental Reading Disorder (classification 315.00). Phil's case file revealed that he started having school-related problems in kindergarten; these problems were severe enough that he was held back and repeated kindergarten. He was described as being frequently off-task when required to work at his desk in the classroom, and he had a reputation for getting into fights on the playground. His mother felt that the school personnel were picking on her son, and she often allowed him to stay home from school even when he was not ill. He had allergies and often complained of headaches. Phil's mother reported that he had experienced health problems at an early age and that he had had several accidents that resulted in broken bones.

When Phil was referred to the Monitor Program, he was living with his mother and stepfather. An older brother had left home two years earlier. Phil's mother reported that he had a problem with his temper; when he was frustrated, he would throw fits that involved punching holes in the walls and breaking furniture. She also said that he had a short attention span except when it came to certain activities, such as playing video games and riding motorcycles.

Phil was not the only family member with a history of aggressiveness. Phil's stepfather, Jim, also was described as having a hot temper. He had been investigated in another county for charges of physically abusing his natural children. Phil's biological father and mother split up when Phil was three years old. Phil and his brother had been physically abused by his father. His mother reported that she "had not been beat on much" by Phil's father. She was worried that Phil had inherited his father's temper. From the time Phil was a toddler until he was 11 years old, Phil and his older brother were jealous of each other and often got into physical fights.

Phil was in detention when he was first interviewed by Monitor Program staff. He smiled broadly throughout most of the interview. When Phil was asked why he was smiling, he said it was because he was nervous. When he was asked about his personal goals and what he thought needed to be changed, Phil said, "I need to take more responsibility for my actions and learn to make better decisions." It was clear, however, that he did not know how to achieve these goals. He had already participated in an anger management program and an intensive school supervision program. Although it was noted that Phil seemed to make progress during the exercises on anger control in class, the skills did not seem to generalize to his behavior outside of class. It was also reported that his parents had not cooperated with the school program. His mother had attended only three family therapy sessions, and his stepfather refused to participate at all; the therapist felt that treatment could not progress without the stepfather's attendance.

The problems Phil experienced while he

was growing up are typical of those reported in the case files of many of the boys accepted into the Monitor Program. When he was a toddler, Phil had persistent problems with noncompliance, aggression, and short attention span. He was frequently involved in physical fights with his older brother as he was growing up, and at least two of the significant adults in his life had modeled the use of violence as a way to deal with problems and stress. Phil's school adjustment was poor from the start, and had been aggravated by frequent absences during the past three years. It was not surprising that Phil was below grade level in both reading and math. Further testing revealed that he did not have any serious learning disabilities.

There were many family issues, including physical abuse, verbal and physical aggression, problems with alcohol, lack of parental supervision, and the stepfather's refusal to participate in treatment. Although Phil's mother had the best intentions and tried to help him, she actually had facilitated the development and maintenance of his problems in many ways. The seriousness of family problems and the severity and escalating nature of Phil's delinquent acts led his court counselor to recommend residential treatment. By the time Phil was referred to the Monitor Program, the situation for Phil and his parents had reached a crisis point. As we will see in the section that follows, the circumstances leading to this crisis had unfolded over the course of Phil's life in a more or less predictable sequence that characterizes the development of antisocial patterns for most delinquent boys.

FROM CONDUCT PROBLEMS TO LATER DELINQUENCY

In their book *Antisocial Boys*, Patterson, Reid, and Dishion (1992) reviewed the empirical literature on variables that have been shown to be correlated with delinquency. Many of these variables have been thought to play a causal role in the etiology of the disorder. Some noteworthy examples include the presence of academic deficiencies (Wilson & Herrnstein 1985), the effect of being labeled as a failure on self-esteem (Schur 1973), peer rejection (Roff 1972; Hartup 1982), and the use of physical punishment by parents (Gleuck & Gleuck 1968; Welsh 1976). Although these and other variables have been reliably related to the presence of delinquency, consistent covariation does not automatically imply causality.

Patterson, Reid, and Dishion argue that sets of specific variables that occur at different stages in the child's development are the keys to understanding the causes of later delinquency. They describe a four-stage sequence that incorporates a number of predictive variables. The stage model also describes patterns of increasingly serious antisocial behavior that gradually unfold over time.

Several caveats must be considered before the model is discussed further. First, it has been pointed out by several authors (Ageton 1983; Chesney-Lind 1988; Berger 1989; Chamberlain 1990) that substantially less research has been conducted on the etiology and treatment of female (versus male) delinquency. The developmental stage model of delinquency described by Patterson and his colleagues is based on data collected on male subjects only. Whether the variables and sequences described in this stage model contribute to the development of female delinquency remains to be examined and tested in longitudinal studies. Second, the model describes a set of processes that evolve over time; these processes usually begin when the child is a toddler. Although it is true that early patterns of antisocial behavior are evident for most severely delinquent boys, these patterns do not apply to a significant subgroup of this population that begin their delinquent careers after the age of 15 or 16 (Patterson, Capaldi, & Bank 1990).

Patterson, Capaldi, and Bank examined hypotheses that tested the relative power of family versus peer influences on early- and late-starting (i.e., first offense at the age of 15 or older) delinquent boys. For the early starters, it was found that family factors, particularly parenting styles, played an important part in the development and maintenance of antisocial behavior during early childhood and that the early antisocial behavior of these boys predicted their later delinquency. In later adolescence (after age 12), peer group influences were shown to overshadow family factors as the variable making the primary contribution to the delinquency process. Late starters, however, are less likely to continue their antisocial patterns into adulthood. These late-starting boys appear to skip stages 1 and 2 of the developmental stage model described in the next section. Therefore, the four-stage model does not adequately explain their initiation or involvement in the delinquency process.

A FOUR-STAGE DEVELOPMENTAL MODEL

Early in the study of families with antisocial children, investigators at OSLC found that they needed to obtain more precise information describing family interactions than they could get by asking parents to describe their child's problems. The strategy employed by Patterson and his colleagues was to conduct a series of observational studies in the homes of families with children referred for conduct problems *and* in the homes of "normal" comparison families. Analyses of the differences that were found to distinguish these two groups have stimulated the development and testing of theories on aggression and delinquency. The resulting four-stage model describes a process that begins with the development of relatively trivial problem behaviors and gradually progresses as the child matures into a broader, more complex and serious array of both covert and overt antisocial behaviors.

Stage 1: Training at Home

Basic training is the label that Patterson uses to describe the first stage. At this point, the preschooler or young child is typically described by his parents as being noncompliant, uncooperative, stubborn, irritable, and difficult to manage in general. During this stage, the child learns that negative reactions to parental requests, such as refusing or arguing, "work" in that parents respond by giving in or backing off. The coercive reactions to parental requests and demands produce immediate rewards from the social environment, in the sense that the child can avoid unpleasant tasks or responsibilities. As young children gradually learn that coercion works, the severity of their noxious behaviors escalates from low-amplitude behaviors (e.g., noncompliance, whining, and talking back) to more intense episodes, including behaviors such as temper tantrums, spitting, and hitting.

The coercion model outlined by Patterson (1982) describes a set of interactional processes that explains the early development and maintenance of children's antisocial behavior in the family. Studies in the homes of these children have shown that their parents are relatively ineffective in teaching or socializing them. Children with conduct problems rarely comply with parental requests, and they engage in high rates of negative behaviors such as arguing, hitting, and temper tantrums. Referred families provide rich schedules of reinforcement for their children's antisocial behavior that can be identified within the interactional sequences of family members (Snyder 1977; Snyder & Patterson 1986). The key mechanisms underlying this basic training for aggression are: (1) the parents' direct reinforcement of the child's negative behaviors, (2) the parents' noncontingent reactions to positive and negative child behaviors, and (3) negative reinforcement sequences.

In negative reinforcement sequences, the child's aversive response to his parents' attempts to set limits or provide discipline is reinforced by the parents' giving up or giving in. The following three-step "dance" is a good example of how this works. The parent tells the child to share a toy with his little brother. The child cries and kicks his brother in reaction to the parent's request. The parent picks up the younger child and removes him, and the older boy is allowed to keep the toy he refused to share. In normal, nonreferred families, approximately 14% of the child's coercive behaviors result in the parent's giving up or giving in; this happens 22% of the time in referred families (Patterson, Capaldi, & Bank 1990). Both experimental and correlational studies have confirmed that negative reinforcement contingencies such as the one just described significantly strengthen the probability of future coercive child behaviors (summarized in Patterson 1982).

Stage 2: The Child Goes to School

During stage 2, the social environment outside the child's home begins to respond to his coercive style. By the time conduct-problem children enter school, they exhibit four times the rate of aversive behaviors as their nonproblem peers (Patterson 1982). It is not surprising that this sets them up for rejection by normal peers (Coie & Kupersmidt 1983) and by teachers (Walker & Close 1992). The basic training for aggression the young child has received at home begins to generalize to the school setting (Ramsey & Walker 1988). Children must be relatively cooperative and compliant to complete even simple classroom tasks. Early failure at following classroom rules leads to the child's being disliked by teachers and peers. Studies on how friendships are formed show that children make decisions about who they like and dislike very quickly (e.g., within the first 30 minutes of contact) and that those initial decisions tend to be quite stable over time. Once a child is disliked by his or her peers, it is difficult to change that negative first impression (Coie & Kupersmidt 1983). The child's abrasive style of interaction also results in rejection by significant adults, such as teachers, coaches, and scout leaders. This means that the child does not benefit from many of the normal socializing experiences, such as participating in games, clubs, or other group activities. This process is described by Patterson, Reid, and Dishion (1992) as follows:

> The antisocial boy does not learn when or how to accept negative feedback through experiences with peers. Because the antisocial boy spends less time participating in organized sports, he quickly falls behind in skills such as throwing a baseball, catching a football, and all of the other activities that are status-related for boys of this age. (p. 118)

Stage 3: Making Friends with Deviant Peers

At stage 3, the combination of antisocial behavior and social skill deficits place the child at increasing risk for involvement with deviant peers. The failure of the parents to properly supervise and discipline their young adolescents provides ample opportunity for them to spend time with peers in similar situations or with older delinquents. Associating with peers who are socially unskilled and who tend to embrace deviant (versus conventional) norms can have a dramatic effect on the life course of a young adolescent.

The longitudinal survey study reported by Elliott, Huizinga, and Ageton (1985) emphasized the strength of the relationship between affiliating with a deviant peer group and later delinquency. They found that those teenagers who had relatively weak bonds with their families and schools and who associated with deviant peers had much greater than expected rates of self-reported delinquent acts (compared with their rates of self-reported delinquent acts prior to associating with deviant peers). They concluded that there was almost no risk for increases in delinquency if there was no reported involvement with delinquent peers, regardless of the youth's level of conventional bonding or strain. In their discussion of the implication of these findings for intervention with delinquents, the authors pointed out that it is ironic that treatments for delinquent youths are often based on group process (e.g., positive peer culture and guided group interaction). These group approaches "may actually be contributing to the maintenance and enhancement of delinquent friendship cliques" (p. 149). In support of the negative effects of group-centered approaches, they cite results of evaluations from street worker programs with delinquent gangs which suggest that the more intensive the services delivered to these groups were, the more delinquent they became (e.g., Klein 1969, 1971; Miller 1962). The evidence for a progression of early antisocial behaviors to delinquency over the course of the child's development is in accord with the findings that such patterns appear to be highly stable over time (Sampson & Laub 1990).

Stage 4: Adult Antisocial Life-styles

Participation in stage 4 describes the career antisocial adult. In addition to their increased risk of incarceration, several longitudinal studies have confirmed that a host of other dire outcomes characterizes this group of individuals (e.g., Caspi, Elder, & Bem 1987; West & Farrington 1973; Robins & Ratcliff 1978–79). Adult problems such as broken relationships, downward mobility (from their parents' SES level), hospitalization for mental health problems, accidents, and alcoholism are a few of the more common outcomes for this population.

CHARACTERISTICS OF MONITOR PROGRAM YOUTHS

The adolescents referred to the Monitor Program tend to come from families in which normal functioning has been impaired by stressors such as poverty, health or mental health problems of parents, and social isolation. The teenagers have often been exposed to multiple parent figures, physical and sexual abuse, family violence, and previous placements outside their homes. They have committed serious crimes that threaten the safety of themselves and others in their communities. One-half of these youths have been arrested for a violent crime (Bank, Chamberlain, & Ray, in preparation).

Table 1.1 summarizes the data on the sex, average age, and family makeup of the first 88 participants in the Monitor Program.

As shown in Table 1.1, slightly less than one-half of the children were living with two parents at the time of referral; in most of the two-parent families, there was one natural parent and a stepparent. Most of the youths referred to the Monitor Program came from families that had been shattered by at least one divorce.

As shown in Table 1.2, most of the adolescents had been exposed to other risk factors, such as poverty, family violence, physical abuse, and sexual abuse.

Monitor Program youths have had an aver-

Table 1.1
Participant Characteristics

Males	(N = 53)
Females	(N = 35)
Average Age (range)	
Males	14.54 (12 – 18)
Females	14.80 (11 – 18)
Number of parents in the home at referral	
2 parents = 48%	
1 parent = 50%	
0 parents = 2%	
Parents divorced	N = 72 (82%)
3 or more siblings	N = 25 (28%)
Youth was adopted	N = 12 (14%)

Table 1.2
Risk Factors

Family at or below poverty level	N = 45 (51%)
Documented family violence	N = 63 (72%)
Child physically abused	N = 39 (44%)
Child sexually abused	N = 23 (26%)

Table 1.3
Incarceration History

Youths with one or more felonies	N = 65 (74%)
Youths adjudicated for sex abuse	N = 8 (9%)
Youths with histories of fire setting	N = 9 (10%)

age of 3.2 previous out-of-home placements (range 0 – 19), including placements in foster care, shelter care, and group homes. Females had an average of 4.3 previous out-of-home placements; males had an average of 2.5 placements. Not surprisingly, 80% (N = 66) had problems with chronic truancy, and less than one-half of these youths were at academic grade level (N = 39, 48%) at the time of referral.

Data on the number of Monitor Program youths with records of serious offenses such as felonies, sexual abuse, and fire setting are presented in Table 1.3. These data highlight the need for close supervision of program youths to protect the community from further criminal behavior.

The statistics in these three tables begin to tell the devastating life stories of these adolescents. Many of them have been neglected or abused by their parents. In other cases, economic stress, illness, or a lack of social support have made it difficult for their parents to provide a stable, nurturing home environment. Tragically, the patterns of antisocial behavior that these teenagers have developed may have been adaptive, given the characteristics of their immediate environments. They have learned how to get what they need and want in the short run. Unfortunately, the long-term effects of early childhood aggression and later delinquency are quite debilitating; early on these children are typically rejected by teachers, normal peers, and their own parents. They have strong convictions that they have been treated unfairly by "the system" and many of the adults with whom they have had contact. In 15% of the cases, the adolescent has made a serious suicide attempt. Drug or alcohol abuse was an issue for 47% of these youths.

MONITOR PROGRAM GOALS

In the Monitor Program, we attempt to change the adolescent's life course by teaching a wide range of skills to both the adolescent and his parents. The teaching focuses on addressing the adolescent's skill deficits and restructuring the family setting. Teaching is most effective in a supportive environment, such as the one provided in the foster home. The foster parents provide close supervision for the child, and they work closely with the program to follow through with treatment goals. Over time, the child learns that arguing and avoidance no longer produce short-term rewards, but compliance and cooperation do. Therapy also is provided for the child's natural parents to help them create a more constructive family setting for the child's eventual return home. Everyone involved in the Monitor Program is faced with the challenge of making significant changes over a relatively short time. It is not surprising that resistance to change and the stress associated with it are part of the treatment process. The myriad of issues involved in setting up the process of change will be discussed in the chapters that follow.

SUMMARY

The adolescents referred to the Monitor Program have serious problems with chronic delinquency. By the time they are admitted to our program, their antisocial attitudes and behaviors have become so well established that their parents often feel nothing can be done to help them. Without intervention, the prognosis for the future adjustment of these adolescents is dismal. Acceptance into the Monitor Program is an opportunity for the youths and their parents to interrupt the processes described in the four-stage model of delinquency presented earlier in this chapter. Our program is designed to help these adolescents be successful, and to build on these successes throughout the placement period and in aftercare.

2

RECRUITMENT, SCREENING, AND PRESERVICE TRAINING OF TREATMENT FOSTER PARENTS

Foster parents are the key agents in the delivery of the child's treatment plan. They must be willing to work as members of a treatment team and be capable of implementing the child's daily program in their home. Many potential foster parents are not appropriate for this program: They may be inexperienced in dealing with teenagers, have strong religious beliefs that supersede program goals, have a great deal of love to give and feel that should be sufficient to overcome the child's problems, disagree substantially with important elements of the program, or prefer to work independently. We strive to recruit strong families in terms of both stability and family management skills.

The salient characteristics of foster parents who have participated in the Monitor Program are discussed in the section that follows. It should be noted that as professionals in the residential and foster care field, we are still lacking scientifically-based methods for selecting foster parents and matching children with specific foster parents or other residential care placements. The "clinical hunches" presented here are based on almost ten years of experience with foster parent selection. The methods we use to recruit foster parents, a four-stage screening process, and our expectations of Monitor Program TFC parents are described. During the final stage of the screening process, foster parents must successfully complete a Preservice Training Course. An overview of the content of that course also is provided.

CHARACTERISTICS OF SUCCESSFUL FOSTER PARENTS

Research on the identification of specific characteristics of foster parents that predict successful placements has proven to be complex. The variables thought to be clinically important include the match between the foster child and the family, the amount and type of supervision and support given to the foster parents, the foster parents' attitude toward and involvement with the child's natural family, and the type of behavior problems exhibited by the foster child. Some of these clinical "hunches" regarding the characteristics of good foster placements have not been consistently supported by the research that has been conducted on foster parent characteristics.

For example, a carefully conducted study of

145 new foster parents by Cautley and Aldridge (1975) found that no single characteristic of either foster parent was predictive of a successful placement. The authors found that the success of first placements was not reliably influenced by the severity of the child's problem behavior, the amount of crisis intervention provided by the social worker, or the extent to which the natural parents attempted to sabotage or disrupt the placement. Several modest indicators of success were identified, including the following: (1) The age of the foster child in relation to the other children in the home was important. It was best if the foster child was the youngest; if the foster child was the oldest, this was a negative indicator only if several preschool-age children were in the home. (2) The experience of the social worker and the amount of preplacement preparation contributed to a successful outcome. If the father was present in the home, preplacement contact with him was important. (3) Both the mother's and father's "degree of familiarity" with child care, including the extent to which they stayed in contact with their own siblings, was predictive of better outcomes. (4) The foster parents' prompt and appropriate handling of common childhood problems without harsh discipline and their making an effort to understand the child's possible reasons for behaving in a negative way contributed to successful placement. (5) The foster parents' attitude toward supervision, specifically their willingness to listen to suggestions regarding how the child should be handled, was a positive indicator. Foster parents with strong religious beliefs tended to provide less successful placements.

This study is an example of the type of research that is needed to help us improve our placement strategies. The relation of these findings to variables that predict placement success for experienced (versus first-time) foster parents is unknown. Also, it is possible that the normal range of problems found in foster care children was not represented in the sample studied (e.g., perhaps their behavior problems were less severe). These limitations point out the need for further research with various populations of foster parents and youths.

Monitor Program Foster Parents

The parents who have been involved in the Monitor Program are a diverse group in terms of age and social class. Both two-parent families and single parents (including one single father) have participated. The age range of foster parents is from 25 to 65. Some parents have children or adolescents of their own at home; others have finished raising their children. Both working- and middle-class parents have been involved in the program.

Forty-five foster parents have worked with the Monitor Program from 1983 to 1992. Of these, 10 (22%) were clearly unsuccessful; either they quit before the end of the child's placement and the child was moved to another home, or it was decided the child should be moved because the foster parents' performance was not satisfactory. Although every effort is made to avoid them, disruptions such as the ones just described are common in these types of programs. This failure rate of 22% in the Monitor Program compares favorably with reported rates of 50% for regular foster care and 36% for a supported placement program serving difficult adolescents (Hazel 1990; The Kent Family Project).

The homes of the most successful foster parents are characterized by a high level of involvement and support. They provide the child with an atmosphere of consistency and fairness. The parents have a clear sense of what can be realistically expected of the child, and they are quick to give him credit for progress. At the same time, they are willing to correct the child and provide consequences for rule infractions or other problems. They avoid the tendency to personalize his misbehavior (e.g., "How could he do this to me?"), even if it causes them inconvenience or is directed toward them. Successful foster parents are flexible and responsive to the child's treatment needs, and they are understanding of his motivations for acting in a particular way.

To illustrate the differences between successful and unsuccessful treatment foster parents, the case managers and foster parent trainers in the Monitor Program were asked to generate a list of adjectives to describe six sets of foster parents: three who were considered to be outstanding and three who were obvious failures. Outstanding foster parents were described as nurturing, amicable, flexible, having a good sense of humor, consistent, caring, concerned, cooperative, happy, worried, active, committed, and practical. Unsuccessful foster parents were described as severe, opinionated, quiet, private, harried, naive, stubborn, punitive, demanding, inflexible, uncooperative, strict, stressed, and busy.

Although these general descriptions do not provide specific criteria for selecting the best foster parents, the information may be clinically useful. The current approach in the Monitor Program is to match youths with foster families based on demographic considerations and clinical hunches. As Weithorn (1988) pointed out in his APA task force report on residential treatment, there is a virtual absence in the mental health fields of well-developed theoretical rationales that link factors about the child such as diagnosis or prognosis to decisions about placing that child in a residential setting. As it now stands, the "place and hope" strategy (Moore et al., in press) is the only option available until further research identifies the factors that allow for more systematic matching of children to families.

Length of Service

Given our efforts to carefully screen and intensively train Monitor Program foster parents, their length of service in the program is important financially as well as for establishing a group of experienced care providers for Monitor Program youths. In our sample of 45 foster families, 5 foster parents were initially motivated to work with us because they wanted to provide placement for a child they knew who had been referred to the program. Once that placement was completed, they did not intend to continue to work with our program. Our experience with this group has been largely positive: 4 of the families were highly successful placements; in the other family, the child ran away during the first week of placement. Of the remaining 30 successful foster families, 6 (20%) decided to provide service for one child only, 8 (26%) provided two placements, and 16 (53%) have provided from three to eight placements.

Of course, we would like to encourage successful foster parents to continue to work with our program, and we are constantly looking for new ways to improve our working relationship with them. In addition to providing our foster parents with ongoing support and supervision, regular respite, and 24-hour crisis intervention, we use other incentives to show our appreciation, including giving special award certificates for managing particularly difficult situations, paying extra costs associated with the care or treatment of a child, giving a $50 bonus at the end of the placement, and encouraging foster parents to attend clinical and research seminars conducted at OSLC.

RECRUITMENT AND SCREENING

Developing effective recruitment and screening procedures is essential to the viability of any treatment foster care program. The section that follows describes the procedures used in the Monitor Program.

Recruiting Potential Foster Parents

The most reliable method for recruiting foster parents has been placing ads in local newspapers. The ads describe the child needing a placement, the experience required, the support services provided by our program, and the monthly payment to be awarded. We have found that such child-specific advertising is more successful than ads calling for foster parents in general. We try to make our ads lighthearted, eye-catching, and appealing. Two examples of successful ads are reproduced in Figure 2.1. We have found that the response to a newspaper ad depends upon factors such as time of year and the state of the local economy. Our experience has ranged from no responses at all to 75 calls for one ad.

Figure 2.1

ALL-AMERICAN HOME

needed for clean-cut 15-year-old boy from neglected background. Experienced parent(s) preferred. Training, support, $540 per month. Call Kathy after July 4, Oregon Social Learning Center, [Phone #].

HUCK FINN

Twelve-year-old boy with troubled background needs stable foster home with older or no children. Mental health background or similar experience preferred. Training, support, and $700 per month. Call Kathy, Oregon Social Learning Center, [Phone #].

Another method that has worked well for us is to pay experienced Monitor Program foster parents a finder's fee of $100 for recruiting a new family that completes the preservice training phase of the program. In most cases, the families recruited in this manner have worked out well. One drawback, however, is the potential for creating hard feelings between friends or putting the Monitor Program parents in a difficult position if their friends are not successful in the program.

A Four-Step Screening Process

All families that express interest in the program are carefully screened. The first step is to contact each family by telephone and conduct a brief interview. This initial contact is made by a foster parent recruiter who has a friendly attitude and a good understanding of the program and the types of children it serves. The contact the applicant family has with the project recruiter is an important first step in their involvement with the program. In addition to basic qualifications, recruiters are selected for their warm interpersonal style. Parents should not feel that they are being interrogated or negatively evaluated during the screening process. The recruiter openly acknowledges that this is a program for difficult-to-manage teenagers, that the treatment approach is proactive, and that the program is not for everyone. The purpose of the initial telephone interview is to describe the program and collect information from applicants about their family, residence, and past experience.

The second step in the screening process involves sending an application to qualified families and checking their personal references. The application describes the goals and rationale of the Monitor Program, the population of youths served, and the role and duties of treatment foster parents. The parents are asked to provide the following information:

demographic data and income level, three references who are not relatives that the parents have known for at least one year, reasons for expressing interest in the program, qualifications for working with difficult youths, events or behaviors of the youth that would cause them to give up, discipline style, family recreational activities, marital status, the length of marriage and dates of any separations, and the role they would expect the youth to assume in their family. The application itself is a powerful screening device. On the average, only 50% of the applications sent out are returned.

The personal references provided by the family are contacted by telephone and asked a series of questions, including the following:

- In your opinion, would they be competent to be foster parents to a troubled teenager?
- How long have you known them and in what capacity?
- Have you seen them work with children or teenagers?
- How would you say they work together as a couple?
- How do they handle stress?
- How do they get along with co-workers?
- Is there anything in their personal life that you think we should know about that might be relevant to their being foster parents?
- What do you think would be the most difficult aspect of foster parenting for this family?
- What do you see as their particular strengths and weaknesses?
- (If applicable) Please comment on how their own children are doing, if they have had problems in the past, and how you think having a teenager in their home would affect them.
- Describe the activities, hobbies, or interests of family members.
- Do you feel that they would sustain their commitment to a troubled child, or would they give up when the going got rough?

If the family's written application and references are satisfactory, a home visit is scheduled by the foster parent recruiter and a case manager. This is the third step in the screening process. During the home visit, in addition to evaluating the general suitability of the family, the key issue is whether the parents would be likely to function well as part of the treatment team. The family must provide more than acceptance, affection, and security for the adolescent who is placed with them. Because these youths have severe problems, the families must be actively involved in the program, consistent in their approach, and cooperative in working toward the specific behavioral goals that have been established for the adolescent placed with them. All families who qualify at this point are referred to the local branch of the Children's Services Division for a screening of their residence and a criminal history check.

PRESERVICE TRAINING COURSE

A Preservice Training Course is the final step in the screening process for foster parents. The program case manager and an experienced Monitor Program foster parent act as co-leaders for the training sessions. The course takes 12 hours to complete. It is delivered in two 6-hour sessions or four 3-hour sessions, depending on the schedule and preferences of the foster parents; the outline of preservice training that follows is based on four 3-hour sessions. The purpose of preservice training is to give the foster parents a working knowledge of the policies and procedures of the program. This includes a thorough understanding of the daily behavior management system (i.e., using points and the level system) that is implemented for all program youths. Other relevant topics are discussed, such as the possible effects on family relationships of providing a home for a troubled adolescent and methods for helping a child deal with specific problems, such as a history of sexual abuse or drug and alcohol abuse, the goals for working with the child's natural parents, guidelines for home visits, and foster parent expectations. Throughout the preservice training, role-playing exercises are used to illustrate common problems and to demonstrate and practice behavior management methods.

Overview of Sessions

Session 1 gives potential foster parents an overview of the program. They are told they will be involved in all aspects of decision making and treatment planning for the case. They are encouraged to contact the program staff at any time if they have questions or concerns about the child's treatment plan or their role as foster parents. The importance of working as a coordinated treatment team in designing and implementing the child's treatment program is emphasized. The structure of the team and the roles of the various members are explained, including that of the foster parents, the case manager, the child's individual therapist, and the natural family's therapist. It is clearly stated that the outcome of the placement is determined, in large part, by how well the treatment team works together. At the end of Session 1, the foster parents are given a manual that describes the policies and procedures of the program (the manual is reproduced in Appendix 1). They are given two assignments: to write down their basic house rules, and to review the program policies and procedures before coming to the next session.

Session 2 begins with a discussion of the policies and procedures of the program. The topics covered include protecting the child's confidentiality, conducting room searches, urinalysis testing, parole regulations, respite care, home safety issues (e.g., securing firearms, house and car keys, and alcohol), monitoring the child's mail, and rules about contact with the child's natural parents and relatives. The house rules that the parents have written down as part of their homework assignment are then reviewed and revised as necessary to create a specific list that fits each family's living situation. For example, foster parents may have rules about using tools or sporting equipment, areas of their home or property that are off limits, or family routines that occur at certain times of the day (e.g., feeding animals). Some of these considerations may be incorporated into the child's daily point system later in the program.

Next, the rationale for the point system is discussed, and the foster parents are given an overview of the three-level system. The importance of reinforcing appropriate behavior is emphasized throughout the discussion. Specific methods for encouraging positive efforts and teaching prosocial behaviors are discussed and role-played. Then we introduce an approach for confronting negative behavior that is designed to keep problems from escalating (additional information on encouragement and discipline methods is provided in Chapter 3). At the end of the session, the foster parents are given the assignment to practice observing and recording a specific behavior before they come to the next session. They can observe the behavior of a child that they have living with them, a behavior of their spouse, or their own behavior.

Session 3 covers the "nuts and bolts" of implementing a Level 1 point system. The giving and taking of points is demonstrated and practiced in role-plays. In particular, foster parents are taught to look for and reward positive behaviors, no matter how small and insignificant they may seem. Foster parents also learn how to provide immediate consequences for signs of negative behaviors. Methods for dealing with suspected problems (versus known violations) such as stealing or lying are discussed and demonstrated, and the rules and appropriate techniques for supervising the adolescent are carefully reviewed. Finally, parents become familiar with their role in providing information using the Parent Daily Report checklist that is administered over the telephone (Chamberlain & Reid 1987).

In Session 4, the Level 2 and Level 3 point systems are reviewed in detail. Foster parents practice using problem-solving and negotiation skills to resolve issues. Specific problem areas such as sexual abuse, drug and alcohol abuse, learning disabilities, and physical or verbal aggression are discussed. A written agreement between the foster parents and the program that specifies duties and payment is reviewed at the end of the session (the agreement and several additional handouts that are given to foster parents are reproduced in Appendix 2).

During the preservice training, the details of the program become increasingly clear to potential foster parents. This helps define, both for the parents and for us, whether we will be able to work together as a coordinated treatment team. Any major philosophical differences generally become obvious after working with the parents for a few sessions. The training process also clarifies the time commitment required of foster parents. Throughout the preservice training, we assess their willingness to work within our system as active members of a treatment team. Foster parents are encouraged to express their doubts or disagreements with our approach. If these issues cannot be resolved to the mutual satisfaction of Monitor Program staff and the foster family, we do not proceed with a placement.

The Written Agreement

Prior to making a placement, foster parents must sign a written agreement that describes the specific services they are expected to provide, the terms of compensation to them, and insurance and liability issues. The foster parents are asked to provide full-time care and supervision for the youth and to implement and monitor his treatment plan. Foster parents are identified as the key agents of support and change for the child. They agree to cooperate with ongoing supervision, attend weekly meetings with program staff in which they will discuss the progress and problems they are experiencing with the youth, and to monitor him at all times (i.e., they must know where he is, who he is with, what he is doing, and when he will be home). It is specified that the program staff will contact them daily to collect data on the youth's adjustment during the past 24 hours and troubleshoot anticipated problems.

The agreement also stipulates the requirements for the youth's overnight absences from the foster home and procedures for arranging visits between the adolescent and his parent(s) and relatives; in both instances, the foster parents must notify and work with Monitor Program staff to make specific arrangements in advance. The program agrees to provide the foster parents with support, assistance, supervision, and training throughout the placement. It is confirmed that program staff will be available during regular office hours and a list of staff members who are available for 24-hour crisis intervention also will be provided. The details of the compensation the parents will receive also are written into the contract. In 1992, the compensation for foster parents ranged from $700 to $900 per month depending on the foster parent's experience with the program. Payment to foster parents is prorated for placements or terminations that may occur during the month. If, for any reason, the child is absent from the foster home (e.g., due to a home visit, detention, or running away) for 10 days or less, the compensation is continued during that period. In addition, the program grants foster parents a monthly allowance to buy clothes for the youth and provides for incidental expenses, such as fees for school, lessons, or special sporting equipment. The foster parents agree to purchase and maintain adequate insurance coverage to protect themselves against reasonable risks to their car, home, or other possessions. The program does not provide the foster parents with insurance and is not liable for any risks associated with having a youth living in their household. The terms of the agreement begin when the youth is placed in the home and end when the placement is terminated.

GUIDELINES FOR WORKING WITH FOSTER PARENTS

We have adopted a few basic principles for working with Treatment Foster Care parents. As essential members of a treatment team, foster parents are considered to be professionals who work with the therapists and case manager to overcome barriers to successful treatment. It is important to acknowledge the difficulty of their front-line role in dealing with the child on a day-by-day basis. Whenever possible, appointments are scheduled at times that are convenient for them, and transportation is made available if necessary.

The report by Hazel (1990) on the Kent Family Placement Program that provided placements for difficult teenagers described a similar approach to working with foster parents. In that program, foster parents were given enhanced status, higher fees than were customary, and group and caseworker support; in addition, written agreements were used with the teenager, the caseworker, and the teenager's family. Their program also adhered to the four general principles for child placement that were proposed by the 1974 Swedish Commission for Placement of Children: normalization of the child in the community, localization of services, voluntariness, and participation of foster parents in decision making. Hazel added a fifth principle, which was to create an atmosphere of openness and egalitarianism with foster parents.

We find that having an open and egalitarian relationship with foster parents is essential for promoting team spirit between the foster parents and the program staff. Foster parents always are fully informed about the child's history and the problems that can be expected during the placement. In designing interventions for the child, the opinions of the foster parents are essential. Because they are living with the child, they have the most intimate knowledge of the child's day-to-day functioning. Foster parents are encouraged to make suggestions on the targets for and timing of interventions to be used with the child.

The foster parents are asked to provide daily, ongoing data about the child's adjustment at home and in the community. The case manager calls each foster family, using the Parent Daily Report checklist to collect data on the child's performance during the past 24 hours and to help discuss current and anticipated problems (the use of the PDR is discussed in more detail in Chapter 10). The case manager is the coordinator for the case and maintains regular contact with each of the participating therapists, parole and probation officers, and school personnel.

The adolescents who receive placements through the OSLC Treatment Foster Care programs are mandated to participate by the courts — they do not volunteer. The court has determined that these children must be placed outside their homes both for their own welfare and to protect the community from further delinquent behavior. In spite of this, we make every effort before the child is actually placed in a home to induce the referred child and his parents to endorse the idea of participating in the program. Meetings are conducted separately with the referred youth and his parents. During the meeting, the program is carefully explained to them, and their consent to participate is obtained (the consent form is reproduced in Appendix 3). A detailed description of these two initial meetings is provided in Chapter 3 (for the child) and Chapter 4 (for the parents).

SUMMARY

Developing a systematic approach for recruiting and selecting foster parents is an important first step for establishing a Treatment Foster Care program. We have found this to be an ongoing challenge. The procedures outlined in this chapter are intended to provide a starting point for other, similar programs. The four-stage screening process, which includes the Preservice Training Course, is the key to selecting and preparing potential foster parents for their role as active members of a treatment team. It also helps to establish their status as professionals who work with therapists to change the life course of troubled adolescents.

3

Preparing the Adolescent and Foster Parents for the Placement

Before an adolescent is placed in a treatment foster home, it is necessary to prepare the adolescent, the foster parents, and the adolescent's biological or adoptive parents for the transition. The goal is to make sure everyone knows what to expect and to anticipate and address any issues that could interfere with a successful placement. This chapter briefly reviews the steps taken in the Monitor Program to prepare both the adolescent and the foster parents for the placement. The procedures for preparing the child's biological or adoptive parents are discussed in the next chapter. This chapter also provides an overview of the rationale, design, and steps for implementing the level system that creates a structured program for daily behavior management of the teenager in the foster home.

PREPARING THE ADOLESCENT FOR PLACEMENT

Even after a stay in detention, placement of an adolescent outside his or her family home in a treatment program is potentially traumatic. Almost every aspect of the teenager's life changes dramatically, and he has little control over the process or outcome. To minimize the adolescent's anxiety and increase cooperation, it is important to prepare him for the placement. The goal is to make the transition as smooth as possible and to help the teenager accept the program and its goals.

The first step in our model is to have the prospective case manager conduct an interview with the adolescent. In the Monitor Program, this first meeting usually takes place in the local juvenile detention facility. The child's parole officer attends the meeting as well; this makes it possible to review the conditions of the adolescent's parole at the same time. It is essential to create a positive atmosphere for the interview and to present a clear and realistic picture of what will be expected of the adolescent while he is in the program. During the interview, the ground rules of the program and the level system are thoroughly explained.

The ground rules specify, in general terms, what the teenager can and cannot do while he is involved in the program and living in a foster home. The rules include the basic stipulations of the parole agreement and the guidelines imposed by the program. The minimum conditions the adolescent must agree to are that he will (1) be in the custody of the foster parents,

(2) participate in all required program activities including therapy sessions, (3) be accountable for his whereabouts, (4) attend school, and (5) agree not to violate the law. In most cases, the adolescent readily agrees to abide by these conditions and to follow the ground rules.

The level system is introduced to the adolescent as a plan for success that will help him stay on track and also make it easier for adults to notice when things are going well. An example of a Level 1 program is explained to the teenager, and he is asked which parts of the program will be most difficult to comply with. The child is given positive feedback for identifying potential problem areas and is told that he will meet with a therapist once each week so there will be plenty of opportunity to talk about how to handle these issues and any other problems that might come up. It is openly acknowledged that the adolescent is not expected to be perfect while he is in the program, but that when he makes mistakes there will be consequences that are specified beforehand. The teenager is encouraged to negotiate in advance if any of the consequences seem unfair; however, it is clearly stated that once a consequence is given it is too late to negotiate any changes.

During this first meeting, when the program is explained in detail, some adolescents say they cannot "make it" in such a program or that they are not willing to try. In these instances, placement is delayed. The child is asked to think about the specific problems he might have in the program, and a second interview is scheduled within a week or two. The parole officer or other individuals who are responsible for finding a placement are notified and asked to discuss with the adolescent the other options he has for placement. In most instances, once the adolescent realizes that the court will not allow a return home until an out-of-home placement is successfully completed, he agrees to participate in the program.

By the time the initial meeting takes place, or shortly thereafter, the case manager decides which family the child will be placed with. The youth is given a brief description of the family, including who is in the family, where they live, and the hobbies and interests of family members. The information is kept brief, and it is delivered in an upbeat manner. The goal is to relieve some of the youth's anxiety about the upcoming placement.

GETTING THE FOSTER PARENTS READY FOR THE PLACEMENT

We believe that the foster parents should be fully informed about the adolescent before the placement is made final. The foster parents are given the complete case file to read, and the case manager discusses it with them until they are satisfied that they understand the child's situation. Any other information the case manager may have about the adolescent or his family beyond the case file, such as impressions from interviews, is also shared with the foster parents. The questions and concerns expressed by the foster parents are addressed in an open and straightforward manner. This discussion between the prospective foster parents and the case manager can take place in person or over the telephone, in one contact or in several, depending on the number and complexity of issues that need to be addressed. Based on this exchange, the foster parents decide whether they are willing to work with the adolescent. We do not routinely use preplacement visits in our program for the following reasons: (1) We are not convinced that such visits help either the teenager or the foster parents determine whether they can work together, and (2) preplacement visits set the adolescent up for rejection if the foster family decides not to accept the placement.

THE LEVEL SYSTEM

During the adolescent's stay in the program, he gradually progresses through a behavior management system that has three levels. The level system is a structured program designed to be used daily to teach prosocial skills, reinforce appropriate behavior and attitudes, and provide sanctions for behavior problems that are expected to occur during the course of the placement. At each successive level, the adolescent is less closely supervised, and he is given more responsibilities and privileges. The adolescent earns the right to move up to the next level by earning points for appropriate behavior and not losing too many points for misbehavior. The objective is to have the teenager functioning appropriately within the context of a family setting by the end of the placement period.

Underlying Rationale

The structure of the level system provides the basis for the program's therapeutic milieu. The design of this milieu draws on research on the development and treatment of conduct problems, delinquency, and antisocial patterns in children and adolescents. The level system uses explicit reinforcement in the form of points that are used to "buy" privileges, material things, and money. Numerous studies have shown that antisocial children are less responsive to social rewards, such as adult approval (e.g., Herbert et al. 1973), yet they seem to learn as well as their normal counterparts when tangible rewards, such as tokens, food, privileges, or money, are used (Marcus 1972). The same seems to hold true for correcting or disciplining these youths. Social disapproval is much less effective than tangible punishments such as point loss or time out (White, Nielsen, & Johnson 1972). In the level system, the child loses points for misbehavior. Children and adolescents with severe behavior problems, such as delinquency or conduct disorder, have an apparent hyporesponsiveness to both social approval and social disapproval that makes them difficult to treat. The normal "middle-class" mechanisms for shaping child behavior that occur naturally in daily interactions, such as praising, lecturing, and generating feelings of guilt, fail to have much impact.

The level system restructures the foster home environment so that the antisocial child consistently receives tangible rewards and sanctions; these consequences are delivered immediately or soon after the occurrence of the child's prosocial or problem behaviors throughout the day. The level system gradually suppresses the child's misbehavior and at the same time provides encouragement for taking small steps in positive directions. This approach helps the delinquent teenager learn from the consequences of his or her behavior.

This population typically demonstrates low levels of competency in many areas of prosocial functioning. It is well documented that delinquent youths tend to be less skilled than their normal peers in several important areas such as sports and hobbies, academic achievement, job skills, and peer relationships (e.g., Chamberlain & Patterson 1984). These children apparently have not developed the ability to use prosocial strategies to achieve their goals. Instead, they rely on coercive tactics to get what they want and to avoid responsibilities. Their abrasive approach "works" in the short run, but in the long run they are at-risk for rejection by their peers and further social isolation. Antisocial children also tend to be rejected by adults who could teach them prosocial skills. The result of this rejection by both peers and adults is a gradual decrease in the opportunities for socialization and skill development that are readily available to other children. As their behavior becomes more extreme, antisocial children are at-risk for associating with a deviant peer group comprising children like themselves. Patterson (1982) calls this process "deviancy drift"; as the child matures, he or she becomes increasingly deviant and isolated. The level system helps the child overcome skill deficits by systematically providing rewards for prosocial behaviors.

Another salient characteristic of adolescents with severe conduct problems is that they invariably have a strong sense that they have been treated unfairly. Whether it has been by their parents, the police, or their teachers, each of them feels victimized in some way. Of course, there are good reasons for this. After reading the case histories of these children, one cannot help but feel sympathetic to their plight. Many of them were raised in families in which there have been serious mental health problems for generations and legacies of abuse, crime, and disrupted relationships have been passed down as part of the family tradition. Attempting to change the life course of these adolescents while treating them in a way they see as fair is a formidable challenge. Our program addresses the fairness issue by encouraging the child to negotiate for changes in the level system and by providing support for such attempts.

Although it may be tempting to ignore the fairness issue, it is not advisable, because these youths seem almost paranoid in their interpretations of the way others react to them. Family therapist Ivan Boszormenyi-Nagy calls this legacy of unfairness "destructive entitlement." That is, an individual will act out in destructive ways to the extent that he or she feels treated unfairly. Paying too much attention to fairness, however, can compromise the effectiveness of the treatment approach. This issue must be kept in balance with other factors, such as the necessity of teaching the child to obey the rules and expectations of society and helping the child develop the skills to achieve long-term goals and build good relationships with others. These are basic requirements for daily living. The level system, if used correctly, creates a home environment that seems fair to the child while providing the structure necessary to foster the development of prosocial skills.

OVERVIEW OF THE THREE-LEVEL SYSTEM

In the Monitor Program, it usually takes four to six months for the child to progress through all three levels. As we mentioned earlier, each successive level is characterized by less supervision and more privileges and rewards. For example, no unsupervised time is allowed in Level 1, and the points the child earns on any given day are used to buy privileges for the next day. Free time can be purchased with points in Level 2, and the points received for an entire week are used to buy privileges for the next week. Points are no longer used in Level 3; daily ratings of the child's performance earn prespecified amounts of allowance. Advancement from one level to the next is based on reaching criterion for that level. If the child does well, it takes 2 to 3 weeks to advance from Level 1 to Level 2, and 12 to 14 weeks to move from Level 2 to Level 3. The level system as it is presented here is intended to provide general guidelines for developing the youth's individualized program rather than a rigid set of rules that is routinely applied to all cases. The system should be adapted to fit the needs of each individual case. The following section reviews in more detail the basic structure and characteristics of the three levels that we use in the Monitor Program.

Level 1

Level 1 is designed to provide the adolescent with close supervision and immediate reinforcement. The adolescents remains at Level 1 until he earns 2,100 points; this usually takes about three weeks. The specific number of points used as criterion for moving to Level 2 can be adjusted to accommodate the needs of an individual case and other factors discussed later in this chapter. In Level 1, the points the adolescent earns on day one determine the privileges available on day two. The teenager should be able to earn an average of 100 points per day. Earning less than 100 points indicates that the adolescent is having problems, and earning more than 100 points indicates that he is doing well. At Level 1, the teenager is supervised very closely, both at home and at school. The privileges teenagers generally take for granted, such as telephone use, free time with friends, a later bedtime, and an allowance, now must be earned.

Level 2

The teenager is allowed to earn free time and more privileges on Level 2. At this level, the points earned during one week are used to buy privileges for the next week. On the average, the adolescent should be able to earn 700 to 900 points per week. This arrangement helps the adolescent learn to delay gratification, plan ahead, and work toward a goal. Typically, the child stays at Level 2 for four months. During this time, the amount and quality of the privileges are increased as the adolescent's behavior and skills improve, giving him a chance to become increasingly responsible and confident.

On Level 2, the adolescent can "buy" free time with friends (the typical rate is half a point per minute). Even during free time, however, the Monitor Program has specific rules and guidelines for both the foster parents and the adolescent. For example, free-time activities must be planned and fully arranged 24 hours in advance, and the teenager must give the foster parents the names, addresses, and telephone numbers of the friends he will be spending time with. The adolescent is told that the Monitor Program is responsible for knowing where he is at all times and that someone from the program will confirm his whereabouts during free-time activities. Our arrangement with the juvenile court usually includes the stipulation that we will carefully supervise the adolescent so he will not commit additional crimes in the community; therefore, the program must approve all free-time arrangements.

Using the telephone for a specified period of time per day (usually 15 minutes) is another privilege available on Level 2. Earning a later bedtime, an allowance, and other individualized rewards, such as swimming lessons, a movie rental, or use of the foster family's CB radio, are also possible on Level 2. The adolescent advances from Level 2 to Level 3 by buying bonds that cost 25 points each. Twelve bonds are required for promotion to Level 3. Bonds can be purchased only at the rate of one per week. Once the child is on Level 2, he can be demoted to Level 1 for low point days (e.g., earning less than 100 points). Once he is demoted to Level 1, a criterion number of points must be earned on Level 1 (usually 100, which can be earned in one day), and then the child is reinstated to Level 2.

Level 3

Points are not earned or lost on Level 3. Instead, the child's performance in several areas is rated each day as excellent, satisfactory, needing improvement, or unacceptable. The amount of allowance the child receives depends on these daily ratings. The child is required to maintain a budget book that tracks all income and expenses. Basic privileges do not have to be earned on Level 3. Activities must be approved in advance, but do not have to be earned. The program continues to check on the adolescent's activities and whereabouts during his free time on Level 3.

The child must perform reasonably well to stay on Level 3. Two or more ratings of unacceptable during any one day or an unacceptable rating for the same behavior on two consecutive days may result in the child's being demoted to Level 2 for one day to one week, depending on the seriousness of the problem. Throughout the child's placement, law violations, truancy, and drug use automatically result in demotion to Level 1. Serious violations like these are often coupled with an additional consequence (e.g., a work chore, writing essays or sentences) that must be completed before he can return to the previous level.

Privileges and Rewards

Privileges are earned day by day on Level 1 and week by week on Level 2. Certain basic privileges are made readily available on Level 3; others are negotiated on a case-by-case basis. Extra rewards are provided when the child performs specific target behaviors such as completing all math homework for a week or taking a "time out" when he feels tense or angry. The additional rewards range from small items such as something special to eat to larger ones such as music or clothing. These rewards are used throughout the program as incentives for appropriate behavior, particularly in situations that are especially difficult for the child. Rewards are usually earned over several days or weeks; that is, they are usually given for sustained performance rather than for single events.

Effective privileges and rewards have the following characteristics:

1. *They are well defined.* The adolescent should clearly understand the reward or privilege being offered. The goal is to leave as little room for interpretation or misunderstanding as possible. For example, does extra telephone time mean 15 minutes or 30 minutes? Can the telephone be used once or twice a day? Before or after homework is finished?

2. *They fit the teenager's level of maturity and interests.* Having a later bedtime would not be of interest to a boy who usually goes to bed on his own at 10:00. Finding appropriate rewards can be a challenge. Some teenagers might want to earn a model airplane kit; others want a new pair of shoes. Although it is always a good idea to ask the adolescent what he wants, it is relatively common for the response to be "nothing" or "I don't know." It is often more effective to have the foster parent or therapist suggest things that they think the teenager might like.

3. *The privileges or rewards must be affordable and readily available.* Foster parents often fall into the trap of offering something that is difficult for them to provide. One way to deal with this is to limit the number of times per week that the teenager is allowed to pick a given item on the list of privileges. Each privilege or reward should be carefully reviewed with the foster parents before it is offered.

4. *The criteria for the reward should be realistic; that is, the adolescent should be able to achieve it with a reasonable amount of effort.* The criteria should be set by looking at the child's current level of optimum functioning and should provide rewards for small steps in the right direction. Many children and adolescents with chronic conduct problems are thoroughly discouraged and have very low self-esteem. If they think it will take a long-term effort to reach criteria, they may give up early because they know that they cannot make it; when they give up, they may become depressed or begin acting out. The goal is to help them be successful.

Point Fines

On Levels 1 and 2, point fines are imposed for small infractions such as not minding, swearing, talking about delinquent activities, and "poison gas" (sulking, surly behavior). Fines are used for these relatively minor events to keep the adolescent's negative behavior from escalating and to teach him that coercion does not work. An advantage of using fines is that they can be delivered in a way that does not erode the teenager's feelings of success. Treatment foster parents are trained to take away points in a sympathetic and nonhostile way. The adolescent is told in advance that "everybody makes mistakes" and that he should expect to lose a few points every now and then.

The timing of the discipline interaction is important. In his review of the literature on punishment, Parke (1969) concluded that punishment for events that occurred early in a coercive behavior sequence was more effective in suppressing problem behavior than punishment for events occurring late in the sequence. He also found that low-intensity (e.g., nagging, lecturing) punishments given late in the coercive sequence were particularly ineffective in stopping the child's problem behavior. The ineffectiveness of repeated lecturing and scolding also has been demonstrated in classroom studies where it was found that "rule giving" without using back-up contingencies did not change the children's behavior (Becker et al. 1967). Point fines are a form of discipline that, if used correctly, prevent the child's negative behavior from escalating and at the same time help the caregivers avoid lecturing, scolding, and getting involved in ongoing power struggles with the adolescent.

LEVEL SYSTEM CHARTS

Level 1 Charts

The child's daily point chart comprises three classes of items:

1. Items that describe the child's schedule for the day (i.e., what he is supposed to do and when)

2. Items regarding appropriate social behavior

3. Items related to problem behaviors targeted for change in the child's treatment plan

The first two classes of items focus on encouraging prosocial behavior and attitudes, and the third class focuses on decreasing antisocial behavior and attitudes. An example of a Level 1 point chart is shown in Table 3.1a.

The definition and expectations for each item on the chart are written down in behavioral terms. We have found that it is often helpful to include examples. The definition should be specific enough that it is not necessary to rely on judgment or inference. Next, a time deadline is specified for each item, and point values are assigned. It is important to involve the foster parents in this process so their family routines can be incorporated and time lines and definitions adjusted to reflect their situation. Then the chart is carefully reviewed with the teenager, and he is given an opportunity to ask questions or clarify aspects of the system. In the Monitor Program, the case manager presents the point chart to the adolescent on the first day of placement at a meeting with his individual therapist and his foster parents.

For those items that tend to occur throughout the day (e.g., good attitude and maturity), it is a good idea to divide the day into two or three time periods for monitoring purposes (e.g., before noon, afternoon to dinnertime, and dinnertime to bedtime). This encourages the teenager to try again even if he gets off to a bad start, which is a skill characteristically lacking in conduct-problem youth. Antisocial children tend to overgeneralize in interpreting the negative aspects of a given situation, which leads them to give up easily when they encounter a

Table 3.1a
Example of a Level 1 Point Chart — School Days

Behavior	Description	Deadline	Possible Points
Up on time	Out of bed	7:00 am	10
Ready in the morning	Teeth brushed, hair combed, showered, dressed, breakfast fixed, dishes cleaned up	7:30 am	10
Morning clean up	Bed made, dirty clothes put away, room neat, bath towel and wash rag put away	7:45 am	10
Go to school	Go to each class; no tardies or cuts	Per schedule	4 per class
Carry school card	Have teacher sign card; bring it home each day after school	Return by 3:45 pm	2 per signature
Behavior in class	No bad reports; for each full day without a bad report, 4-point bonus	End of school	1 per class (4-pt. bonus)
Homework	50 minutes (does not include letter writing)	7:00 – 7:50 pm	20
Attitude/maturity	Being helpful, taking criticism well, being pleasant, not pushing limits; not being moody	At 1:00 At bedtime	15 15
Volunteering	Volunteering to do extra tasks		2 to 10
Daily chores	To be explained each day; chore takes 10 to 15 minutes	By 6:00 pm	10
Go to bed on time and lights out	If you CAN buy BASICS If you CAN'T buy BASICS	9:30 pm 9:00 pm	10

problem or difficult situation. They also tend to be rigid in their pattern of coercive or negative responding, even though it sets them up for punishment and rejection. The purpose of the level system is to create a setting that provides a range of opportunities for these adolescents to practice adaptive, prosocial responses in family and school settings. The most effective teaching strategy is to consistently reward their positive efforts with both instrumental and social reinforcement. Tables 3.1b, c, and d show examples of other Level 1 charts: a privilege list, hints for earning points, and a list of possible fines.

Table 3.1b
Example of a Level 1 Privilege List

Privilege	Description	Cost in Points
Basics*	Listen to the radio in your room; 9:30 bedtime	60
TV	Can watch TV *with permission* after studying, reading, and chores are done	30
Other	Use of weights and weight room equipment	10
Later bedtime	11:00 pm — Friday, Saturday, and holidays	20

Basics must be purchased before you are eligible for other privileges

Table 3.1c
Hints for Earning Points

1.	Saying please and thank you at appropriate times (showing appreciation).
2.	Offering to help when you see that someone is busy.
3.	Saying something positive to someone else.
4.	Asking for help instead of becoming frustrated and angry.
5.	Taking responsibility for doing your chores, reading, and study time without being reminded.
6.	Not arguing.
7.	Minding within a resonable period of time.
8.	
9.	

Table 3.1d
Possible Fines on Level 1

Behavior	Example	Cost in Points
Missing a class at school*		20
Being tardy to class		10
Poor behavior in school		10 per report
Not turning in assignments		2 to 10
"Poison gas"	Sulking, glaring, not answering when spoken to, etc.	2 to 10
Talking about illegal things	Talking about any illegal behavior, including drug and alcohol use	2 to 10
Swearing	Any profanity	2 to 10
Using put-downs or threats	Nasty or rude talk, or saying you will do something bad	5 to 50
Back talk or arguing		2 to 30
Not minding	Just not doing what you were told to do	2 to 25
Unsupervised time*	Not telling foster parent where you are going and/or not being where you are supposed to be	1 per minute
House rule violations	Not following house rules regarding other people's things; using other people's things without permission	2 to 50
Suspicion of lying		2 to 50
Suspicion of law violation*	Vandalism, shoplifting, etc.	determined by case manager
Stealing*	Leaving the house with other people's possessions; coming home with something that is not yours; reports from others that you are suspected of stealing	5 to 50

Foster parents are required to contact case manager immediately following these incidents.

Level 2 Point Chart

As shown in Table 3.2a, privileges are purchased for a week at a time on Level 2. The assignment of points and privileges on Level 2 is more dynamic than on Level 1; the number of points required to buy privileges is adjusted to reflect weekly fluctuations in points earned, and new privileges are added when appropriate. This fine-tuning ensures that the level system keeps pace with changes in the adolescent's interests and increasing competencies, and it keeps him interested and engaged in the process.

The therapist works with the adolescent to propose new privileges to add to the list; we use this process as an opportunity to help the teenager develop the prosocial skill of asking when he wants something and to help him learn and practice negotiation skills. The adolescent is encouraged to pursue a hobby, sport, or interest by making relevant privileges available on the point chart (e.g., fitness club passes, soccer camp, ski trips). Typically, as the adolescent progresses through Level 2, the point system is adjusted so standard items such as basic privileges, TV, telephone, and free time cost relatively fewer points to buy and other special privileges are added to the list. It is important to make sure that the Level 2 privilege list does not remain static over time. An example of a Level 2 privilege list is shown in Table 3.2b.

Table 3.2a
Example of a Level 2 Point Chart – Nonschool Day

Behavior	Description	Deadline	Possible Points
Up on time	Out of bed	8:30 am	10
Ready in the morning	Teeth brushed, hair combed, showered, dressed, breakfast fixed, dishes cleaned up	8:45 am	10
Morning clean up	Bed made, dirty clothes put away, room neat, bath towel and wash rag put away	9:00 am	10
Chore – morning Chore – evening	To be explained each day	By 1:00 pm By bedtime	10 10
Attitude/Maturity	Being helpful, taking criticism well, being pleasant, not pushing limits; not being moody	At 1:00 pm At bedtime	15 15
Volunteering	Volunteering to do extra tasks		2 to 10
Extra chore	Optional		5 to 50
Hearing no and not arguing	When told to do something by your parents or told no, you do not argue and accept what they say by minding or not saying anything		10
Time Out	Taking a time out when angry		15
Go to bed on time and lights out	If you CAN buy BASICS If you CAN'T buy BASICS	11:00 pm 9:30 pm	10
TOTAL			**175**

Child must earn 100 points for the day to stay on Level 2. He can earn 2 hours free time for the next day.

Table 3.2b
Example of a Level 2 Privilege List

Privilege	Description	Cost in Points
Basics*	Use of telephone for 15 minutes once a day; listen to radio in your room; 9:30 pm bedtime	350
TV	Can watch TV after homework and chores are completed	100
Later bedtime	11:00 pm bedtime — Friday, Saturday, and holidays	40
Extra telephone time	One 20-minute phone call (not long-distance)	25
Free time	With prior permission and approval, you can plan to go to a friend's house, sports events, school activity, for a walk, bike ride, etc. Overnight activities are to be negotiated. You must make your plans 24 hours in advance.	1/2 point per minute. *Maximum* 2 hours free time per week
	Having a friend over.	1/4 point per minute
Personal purchases	$5.00 per week to be used for purchasing records, tapes, or clothing. Must have receipts for all purchases.	200
Other		
Bonds	1 bond costs 100 points 6 bonds, and you advance to Level 3	50 points per week (max.) toward bonds

Basics must be purchased before you are eligible for other privileges.

Level 3 Chart

Major structural changes take place in the adolescent's program on Level 3. As shown in Table 3.3a, the teenager is rated in several areas each day, and money is earned (not privileges) based on these ratings. The rating categories are generally more global than the point chart categories were on Levels 1 and 2.

It is no longer necessary for the adolescent to earn the standard items (e.g., basic privileges, TV, telephone, later bedtime, and free time for activities). As shown in Table 3.3b, the adolescent is expected to keep track of the amount of money he earns and spends each day. Plans for free time must still be approved in advance. In certain cases, the structure of Level 3 is modified to retain certain features of Level 2, such as defining performance expectations in behavioral terms. In addition, Level 3 should be structured to fit the program that will be implemented in the child's home or other aftercare placement; this strategy minimizes transition problems.

POINT SYSTEM ECONOMY

The economy of the point system must be both realistic and balanced for it to work. The overall design of the economy has important implications for treatment outcome. The system should be set up so the adolescent feels successful even when he does not earn all the possible points. It should offer the adolescent both material things and a life style he wants to earn. If the level system is used correctly, it becomes a motivating force throughout the TFC placement. It also helps the teenager become accustomed to receiving both positive and negative feedback on his behavior.

Table 3.3a
Example of a Level 3 Chart

Name _____ Week of _____

	Mon	Tue	Wed	Thu	Fri	Sat	Sun
Social							
Attitude/maturity							
Accepting responsibility							
Attention to tasks							
Being considerate of others							
Planning							
Courteous approach							
Mature negotiating							
Home							
Chores							
Volunteering							
Quality of work							
Being responsible							
Personal belongings							
Communication with small children							
Independent Living Skills							
Personal care							
Following doctor's directions							
Following foster parents' directions							
Budgeting							
Receipts							
Preplanning*							
Attitude/maturity							
School							
Grades							
Attendance							
Social behavior in school							
Positive approach							
Homework/study time							
Community							
No calls or reports from others							
No parole violations							
No illegal activity							

* *All plans must be arranged and approved 24 hours in advance.*

Table 3.3b
Budgeting and Expenses on Level 3

1. Keep track of the amount of money you earn each day.
2. Keep track of how much you spend each day.
3. Keep track of what you spend it on.
Two **UNACCEPTABLE** ratings on any given day = automatic demotion to Level 1.
One **UNACCEPTABLE** rating on two days in a row = automatic demotion to Level 1.
Expenses
You are responsible for all personal expenses for recreation and special clothing.
I have read and understatnd the conditions of Level 3.
Name _____ Date _____

Assigning Point Values

Several factors must be taken into consideration when assigning point values for a task or behavior. How difficult is the task or behavior? Is it something particularly difficult for this individual? Does the teenager have a good chance of being successful? How important is it for the adolescent to succeed? How fair will a given point value seem? Ideally, the adolescent should be able to lose 10 – 20 points per day without having his privileges seriously curtailed. Typically, the adolescent can earn a maximum of approximately 150 points each day; this includes options to work for additional points to purchase special privileges. Full points are awarded for doing an adequate (but not exceptional) job, and partial points are given for doing only part of a job. In addition, the foster parents are encouraged to spontaneously give a small number of "extra" points if they observe the adolescent acting in an especially positive way or handling a difficult situation well.

Giving and Taking Points

The foster parents are trained to administer the point system in a way that is both firm and fair. It requires considerable skill on the part of the parents to achieve this balance. The adolescent should feel successful when points are given, and when points are taken away it should be communicated in a neutral or compassionate way so that the teenager's feelings of failure or discouragement do not interfere with his future performance. In most instances, points are taken away at the time of the infraction. Usually one or two points are deducted for routine problem behaviors such as pouting, swearing, and talking back. When points are removed, the adolescent will often test the foster parents' commitment to the program and try to sidetrack them to keep them from following through. The parents are taught to avoid engaging in long discussions or offering detailed explanations about why it is necessary to deduct points for the infraction. The adolescent is told that if he thinks the consequence is unfair, it can be discussed at another time. The goal is for the parents to be both firm and fair.

Parents who tend to be irritable, avoid conflict, or personalize the child's failures will have difficulty using this system. The program is demanding for caretakers in the sense that they are expected to maintain control over their own emotional reactions and respond to the child's behavior in a systematic manner. It is often tempting and perhaps more satisfying for the foster parent to lecture or yell about a recurring problem instead of taking points away. To the extent that the parents are invested in the child's success, they may personalize the child's misbehavior and think, "How could he do this to me?" Another common trap is for foster parents to "overlook" minor infractions and not take the required number of points away. If this happens, when the teenager misbehaves in the same way again, the foster parent is likely to become angry and overreact by arguing, lecturing, or taking away more points than is warranted.

Reviewing the Point Chart

Each evening, one or both foster parents should review the point chart with the teenager for 5 to 10 minutes. The purpose is to give encouragement by focusing on the positive aspects of the teenager's performance during the day, to help resolve issues, and to review strategies that will help him avoid losing points the next day. It is important for the foster parents to discuss the point chart at the end of the day instead putting it off until later. This can be especially problematic when the adolescent has had a bad day and has lost several points; if the point chart is reviewed the next morning, the teenager will start the new day feeling discouraged, which may result in continued problems.

Rewards

Special rewards are often effective for changing problem behaviors that occur frequently or that are especially disruptive to the adolescent's development or success in the program. These rewards are usually earned over a period of days for a series of successes. Avoid using rewards for behaviors that are difficult to observe (e.g., not stealing, not using drugs). One approach that we have found to be particularly effective is to engage adolescents in challenges or "bets." The following case example demonstrates how this technique was used with Brian, a 15-year-old boy who was referred to our program.

CASE EXAMPLE: BRIAN AND THE BET

When Brian was asked why he kept running away from the group home, he replied that it was usually an impulsive, spur-of-the-moment decision. He said that he did not plan to run away in advance. He said that he had liked the staff and the conditions at the group home. Nonetheless, he had been in the group home for just three weeks when he ran away the first time, and by the fourth week he had run away two more times. Brian was described as having a history of detachment and lack of bonding with parental figures. He had been placed in foster care as an infant. He was adopted at age four, after several different foster placements. At age seven, his adoptive parents divorced, and he went to live with his adoptive mother. She remarried one year later and was soon pregnant. Brian, who had problems with inattentiveness and impulsivity, began to fail in school and act out at home. He was also disruptive at home and was challenging his mother's authority. Finally, he was sent to live with his adoptive father, who had just remarried. Brian's problems continued and became more severe; he was arrested for stealing and then for a series of burglaries. After several arrests, he was ordered by the court to be placed in the group home. After his failure there, he was returned to locked detention and eventually placed in the Monitor Program.

At the first clinical staff meeting after Brian was admitted to the program, the team expressed concern that he would run away again. It was obvious that Brain needed an intervention that would prevent him from running away from the foster home. Brian's lack of attachment or bonding with parental figures also would have to be addressed because this seemed to be related to his pattern of running away. How could we keep this boy in the foster home long enough to allow us to put the treatment program into effect? After several options were discussed, it was suggested we could try to work on getting Brian attached by building on his relationship with his individual therapist (BK). BK had made a good initial connection with Brian, so we decided to use this relationship to try to keep Brian in the program.

BK told Brian that the Monitor Program staff had talked about whether Brian was going to run away, and that most of the other staff members thought Brian would not be able to make a commitment to the program. BK told Brian that he had disagreed and said that he thought Brain "had what it took" to finish the program. The other program staff said that BK was crazy or at least naive. BK then told Brian that "in an impulsive moment I *bet* the program director $15 that you would stay around for at least the next month."

BK then appealed to Brian to help him out. BK said that he could not afford to lose the $15 and emphasized that he would lose face and credibility with the other program staff members if he was wrong about Brian. BK then offered to split the money with Brian if he did not run away. The idea was that Brian might succeed if he was given a reason or purpose outside himself to resist the temptation to run away. We were counting on the relationship that Brian had with his therapist and the additional incentive of a monetary reward to change Brian's pattern of running away.

The intervention worked. Brian made it for four weeks with no problems, and Brian and his therapist took the bet money they had won and spent it on a movie and a meal that they shared. The therapist emphasized to Brian how pleased he was that he could count on Brian, and that this showed him Brian could follow through when he put his mind to it. At this point, Brian had stayed in the program without any AWOLs, and he had made it to Level 2.

A Small Backfire

Unintended consequences are often associated with an intervention, particularly if it has had an effect. Part of the clinical problem-solving process is to anticipate these outcomes and develop responses that reframe problems as part of the child's treatment plan. However, there are surprises sometimes. In this case, we had not anticipated that Brian would brag to his father about how he had gotten $15 out of the program.

Brian's father strongly objected to what we had done. He told the family therapist who was assigned to the case (MSF) that he felt it was unprofessional of BK to have made a bet. He said it made Brian feel that he had conned the program. MSF explained the purpose of the intervention and told the father that Brian had not conned the program but in fact had been set up to "win" the bet. She reframed the father's objection by telling him it gave Brian an opportunity to feel successful for sticking with his commitment to BK.

Family Treatment

Although the goals and methods of family treatment are described in the next chapter, a brief overview of the treatment for Brian's family is given here. From the outset, Brian's adoptive father told MSF he thought that Brian was certain to fail in the program. He said Brian had not bonded with anyone since the adoption, and he felt that Brian should not be returned to live with him again. Brian's adoptive mother had also said that she was unable to have Brian live with her. The case was at-risk for a disrupted adoption. As in many cases such as this, if the adoption failed, it would have been very difficult to find a long-term placement for Brian due to his history of recurring problems and his age.

In joint sessions with the father and Brian, MSF had observed that the father and boy primarily had negative exchanges with each other. Their range of options for relating to each other, in terms of content and affect, seemed quite limited. For example, even when the father tried to be reinforcing to his son, his affect was both avoidant and angry; he would look away from Brian and use a hostile or disgusted tone of voice. In his father's presence, Brian bragged and exaggerated his own accomplishments.

In individual sessions and telephone contacts with the father, MSF was understanding and sympathetic in response to his concerns about Brian's ability to complete the program and to live at home with the father and stepmother afterward. Eventually, MSF challenged the father by saying, "It sounds like you want to give up before we even have a chance to get started with the program." The father replied that he did not want to give up on Brain before he failed, but that this was Brian's "last chance." MSF suggested that they put long-term placement decisions aside for a period of time while MSF worked with the father, stepmother, and Brian to help them learn and practice using positive communication skills when they interacted with one another in the therapy sessions.

Over several months they worked on a series of basic skills such as paraphrasing, stating topics in neutral terms, and using negotiation and problem-solving strategies. Once the basic skills were in place, MSF used naturally occurring events to have Brian, his dad, and his stepmother practice the new skills. Some of these events were occasions when Brian had a problem.

For example, about midway through the program, Brian was suspended from school for smoking. The case manager and MSF, in consultation with BK and the TFC parents, came up with a plan to use these instances to build family skills that would allow the parents and Brian to live together successfully even when Brian had problems. It was decided that Brian should tell his father the "bad news" about being suspended from school. BK and Brian prepared by rehearsing how Brian could tell his dad about this difficult situation. BK advised Brian to state neutrally and plainly that he had smoked on school grounds and to take responsibility for "messing up." MSF worked with the father to help him learn to respond in a nonhostile way and give a reasonable consequence for problem behavior.

In a joint session, Brian told his father about his problem. The father responded neutrally and discussed with MSF what he thought an appropriate consequence should be. They agreed that Brian would have to be supervised while he did schoolwork at home during normal school hours, and that he would be demoted to Level 1 with no free time or telephone privileges until he was back in school. The case manager worked with the TFC parents to help them follow through with the consequences as planned.

These family interventions were a crucial part of the treatment plan for Brian. Along with several others, they laid the groundwork for family change that eventually (i.e., after six months) made it possible for Brian to live with his adoptive father and stepmother. As Brian's return home became imminent, the father and stepmother began to use small consequences during Brian's home visits, and they set up a point program. They continued to use a modified level system with Brian when he returned home. After Brian left the Monitor Program, they continued to receive family treatment for six months, and the stepmother attended the aftercare parent group (described in Chapter 8). Brian is currently in the Job Corps, a vocational training program, where he is working and learning to become an automobile mechanic. He lives in a neighboring state and returns home regularly for visits.

SUMMARY

One of the primary advantages of the TFC model over group care is that the treatment plan can be customized to fit the needs of the individual. The level system is compatible with the TFC model because it is both effective and easy to modify. We design a daily behavior management program for each case using the basic template for points and levels described in this chapter. This template is adjusted to make the program more clinically relevant by adding well-defined target behaviors to the adolescent's daily point program. These additions can be suggested by any member of the treatment team, and the case manager usually takes the lead in discussing program modifications with the TFC parents and individual and family therapists so everyone is "on board." Examples of individualized targets include the following: practicing specific social behaviors (e.g., using good table manners, being verbally polite, asking about someone else's well-being), appropriately expressing one's feelings or needs (e.g., asking for help, asking for reassurance, expressing likes and dislikes), practicing self-control (e.g., being patient, taking a break when tense or angry), and demonstrating sustained performance at a difficult task or in an area in which the adolescent had previously failed. The extent to which the system can be customized is limited only by the creativity, energy, and resources available within the program. Individualization is the cornerstone of a well-run TFC program, and it is one of the primary benefits for its participants and their families.

4

FAMILY TREATMENT FOR THE CHILD'S BIOLOGICAL OR ADOPTIVE PARENTS

The TFC model developed at OSLC emphasizes the importance of preparing the family for the child's eventual return home. The focus is on providing training and support for a child's biological or adoptive parents. Siblings and other relatives are also integrated into the family treatment plan when it is appropriate. The long-term goal is to put the child's natural family in a better position to help the child live successfully at home. This means the parents must change the way the family functions. To accomplish this, parents need support and encouragement in addition to intensive training in specific parenting skills. These skills typically include using discipline effectively, providing adequate supervision for the child, reinforcing the child's prosocial behaviors and skills, and improving communication and problem-solving strategies. This chapter reviews the approach used in the Monitor Program to develop a good working relationship with the parents, provide support, and teach them new skills.

ESTABLISHING A WORKING RELATIONSHIP

To work effectively with the parents, it is essential for the therapist build an alliance with them. The therapist and parents must learn to work together as a team to identify and implement the appropriate changes for the child. The first step toward this goal is to understand how the parents view the situation. This may be difficult if the therapist has a different perspective regarding what has caused the child's problems and the changes that must take place in the family. In successful cases, however, the perspective or "story line" of the parents and that of the therapist merge over time (Patterson, personal communication, 1990), reflecting an integration of the two. Initially, the therapist should validate the feelings of the parents and empathize with their situation rather than trying to convince them that he or she has a better understanding of what is going on in their family.

From the outset, the parents usually feel alienated and disempowered by "the system." Most of them have a history of involvement with social service agencies and the court and are understandably apprehensive about the prospect of another contact. In addition to their anxiety about being blamed for their child's problems, the thought of devoting time to family therapy is unpleasant for them, and the weekly sessions are usually regarded as one more source of stress they must endure. Frustrated by their inability to manage their child's behavior, they are negative about the child's chances of success in the program. Many are distraught about the placement itself. Although placing their adolescent in the Monitor Program usually gives the parents some relief from the chaos in their family, having their child removed from the home strikes a deep chord in many of these parents, and it further disrupts the family.

The first four tasks for the family therapist are to:

1. Build a supportive, trusting relationship with the parents

2. Ask the parents to describe past events and current factors that may be related to their child's problems

3. Assess the strengths of the parents, their relationship with their child(ren), and the extent of their social support network

4. Help the parents understand the treatment model the program will use to work with their child

All four of these initial tasks have a positive focus. Together, they build the foundation for a successful treatment outcome. Another important strategy is to avoid having confrontations with the parents during the first several sessions. This can be difficult if the parents resist treatment, which is often the case in the Monitor Program. Some common barriers presented by parents include problems with scheduling, failing to show up for appointments, and being late to initial therapy sessions. During the sessions, parents might be hostile to the therapist or suggest the situation is so hopeless that nothing can be done. Any one of these reactions can sidetrack the therapist. It is the therapist's job to make contact with the parents (i.e., establish a therapeutic relationship) and maintain a good working relationship with them as the treatment progresses.

Sometimes it takes several telephone contacts or home visits before the parents will agree to participate in the treatment sessions. The parents are given several options, depending on their circumstances. One option is to have them come to OSLC for their family therapy sessions; to make this easier, funds are set aside in the Monitor Program to pay for transportation. Another option is to conduct the treatment sessions in the parents' home; this arrangement seems to work best for many of our families. When parents refuse to attend therapy sessions, we assume it is our responsibility to solve the problem. By offering several options and working to identify and remove barriers to parent participation, we are successful in engaging almost all parents in family treatment.

Research on Resistance to Family Therapy

After almost 20 years of conducting treatment studies on families with conduct-problem children, a group of researchers and therapists at the Oregon Social Learning Center decided to take a systematic look at the cases that failed to respond to treatment. The subjects for the studies were families referred for treatment because their children were aggressive or antisocial. A series of studies were conducted to examine client – therapist interactions and their relation to case outcomes (Chamberlain et al. 1984) and to changes in parenting that did or did not take place in the family (Forgatch 1991).

Two codes were developed to study therapist and client behavior during the sessions. The codes were modeled after the Family Interaction Coding System (FICS) developed in the 1960s to collect data on the ongoing, moment-by-moment interactions among family members (Reid 1978). The new code categories were conceptualized by observing videotapes of family therapy sessions, discussing specific cases, integrating clinical theories, and reviewing the literature on therapy process.

The code categories for the client and the therapist are listed in Table 4.1. The categories were designed to be relatively simple and straightforward so the codes could be used with a minimum of inference. Research assistants were trained to use the codes at an acceptable level of reliability, which was monitored throughout the research.

One of the most interesting findings from these studies was the way in which therapist and client influenced each other from one interaction to the next. For example, Patterson and Forgatch (1985) found that there were immediate increases in client resistance when the therapist engaged in teaching or confronting behaviors. By contrast, the therapist's supportive statements were associated with immediate decreases in resistance. The code category "Teaching" included all instances in which the therapist referred to parenting practices. It is probably not surprising that parents involved in family treatment react negatively to being asked to discuss or change the way they supervise, discipline, or encourage their children. Yet these are the aspects of family life that have been shown to be related to the development of antisocial behavior in young children and adolescents (Laub & Sampson 1988; McCord 1979; Patterson 1986).

Client behavior also influenced the therapists. For example, it was found that high levels of parental resistance during the middle sessions of treatment were associated with a shorter length of treatment and lower ratings by the therapists regarding how much they liked the parents (Patterson, Dishion, & Chamber-

Table 4.1
Therapy Process Content Codes

Categories for Coding Therapist Behaviors
1. Supporting/Empathizing: positive responses directed at the client that show warmth, humor, understanding, or encouragement
2. Teaching: giving instruction, suggesting what to do and how to do it; includes giving and reviewing homework assignmnents and providing rationales
3. Structuring: establishing the direction of the session by guiding the conversation or activities
4. Interpreting/Reframing: speculating, making predictions, using metaphors or analogies
5. Disagreeing/Confronting: disagreeing, showing disapproval, expressing disbelief, indirect confrontation
6. Facilitating: short utterances that indicate listening or encourage the client to continue talking
Categories for Coding Parent Behavior
1. Disagreeing/Confronting: indicating dissatisfaction with the therapist or therapy, or disagreeing with the therapist
2. Defending: justifying, making excuses, or forgiving your own problem behavior, or the child's, or someone else's
3. Hopeless/Blaming: making statements about not being able to change, having a defeatist attitude, being demoralized, complaining, blaming others
4. Nonresisting: making neutral or cooperative statements, describing events or conditions, discussing, problem solving, talking

lain 1993); interestingly enough, this subgroup of parents also tended to have higher scores for depression at baseline. Two other variables shown to be related to higher initial levels of parental resistance and dropping out of treatment included agency referral (versus self-referral) and having an older (versus younger) target child. Furthermore, it was observed that successful cases were characterized by the specific pattern of resistance illustrated in Figure 4.1. For successful cases, parental resistance peaked at midpoint and then dropped to baseline levels at termination.

The findings from these studies have important implications for the treatment of families with antisocial children. First, the therapist should not expect the parents to be open and cooperative during the initial treatment sessions. In fact, parents spend from 6% to 22% of their time in the first few sessions saying that the treatment will not work; by the middle sessions of treatment, this figure increases to

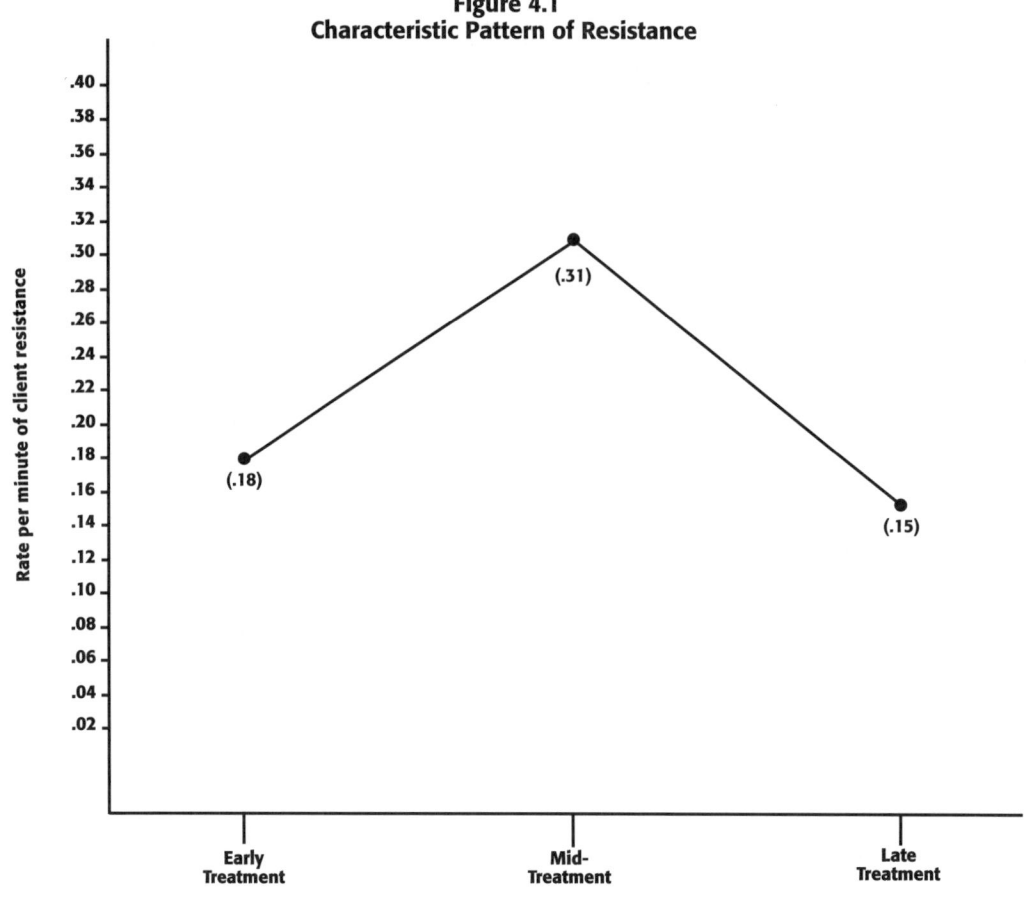

**Figure 4.1
Characteristic Pattern of Resistance**

Source: Chamberlain et al. 1984, p. 150. Reprinted with permission.

approximately 30%. This increase in resistance might be due to the treatment agenda for the middle sessions. In the OSLC model, it is usually at this phase of treatment that the therapist helps the parents work on their discipline skills. From the parents' perspective, one of the most difficult aspects of our treatment model is being asked to change their style of using discipline. This is particularly salient for parents with children who are older or extremely antisocial because the parents have experienced more failures in their discipline attempts. The therapist must begin by convincing these parents that they can use discipline successfully if they change their approach.

The data from these studies point to an obvious need for the therapist to achieve a balance between teaching and being supportive during the treatment sessions. If the therapist fails to teach, it is unlikely that the parents will change the way they deal with their child's conduct problems. A number of studies examining the effects of therapy approaches that provide only support have shown little or no change in the child's problem behaviors (e.g., Walters and Gilmore 1973). The ideal balance between teaching and support probably varies from case to case. In pilot analyses, we have found that inexperienced therapists tend to teach more often and for longer periods than do experienced therapists. Experienced therapists are more parsimonious and strategic with their attempts to teach.

In a study described in detail in Chamberlain and Ray (1988), OSLC therapists who were experienced in the treatment model spent approximately 20% of all session time teaching. A sample of therapists using the Structural Family Therapy (SFT) approach spent approximately one-half as much time teaching. In addition, differences were noted in the rates of confronting behavior for the two approaches: During the initial sessions, OSLC therapists spent one-third as much time as SFT therapists engaging in confronting behavior (2% versus 6% of the session). The difference was less extreme but still noticeable at midtreatment; OSLC therapists engaged in this behavior approximately one-half as much as SFT therapists (4% versus 7%). During the final stages of treatment, the rate of confronting behavior was the same for both OSLC and SFT therapists (6%). It was mentioned earlier that most of the parents involved in the Monitor Program have had a series of negative contacts with social service agencies, the juvenile court, and therapists. We have found that it is not productive to be confrontive with these parents, especially during the initial phases of treatment.

Therapists using a relatively directive approach in their work with families of antisocial children and teenagers can expect to encounter parental resistance when they make suggestions for change. In fact, Patterson, Dishion, and Chamberlain (1993) hypothesized that treatment will not progress without a struggle between the therapist and the client — if the parents are serious in their attempts to change some aspects of their family life, they will present challenges to their therapist.

SETTING UP THE PLACEMENT

Typically, the case manager conducts the preplacement meeting with the parents. After that, the family therapist meets with the parents once each week for the duration of the child's placement in the program. During these meetings, the therapist works intensively with the parents to teach them family management skills. The parents are taught specific skills in the context of a behavior management system that parallels the daily point system being implemented with their child in the foster home. The goal is to have the parents use a simplified version of the point program when their child comes home for visits. Regular home visits are scheduled on weekends or holidays throughout the placement. These visits ensure that the parents continue to have contact with their child and provide opportunities for them to practice using the behavior management skills they have learned in the family therapy sessions.

The Preplacement Interview

Before the child is placed in a foster home, the case manager meets with the child's parents or relatives and conducts the preplacement interview. The case manager begins by describing the basic structure and goals of the program. The relationship of the program to the court, Children's Services Division, and the child's school is thoroughly explained. Then the individual and family treatment components are discussed, and the daily point system is reviewed. The case manager also reports on the experience, training, and supervision of the foster parents with whom the child will be placed. Throughout the discussion, the child's parents or relatives are encouraged to ask questions.

It is essential for the case manager to establish a positive working relationship with the parents during the first interview. This is the first step toward overcoming the parents' resistance to treatment, which can be considerable, as mentioned earlier. The parents are told that their input is welcome and that their child's success will largely depend on how well they work with the TFC program staff to help the child change his patterns of antisocial and delinquent behavior.

At this point, most parents are discouraged and upset. They often say that they have "already tried everything" to help their child and that nothing will work. In this situation, the case manager should assume a nonblaming attitude and convey an interest in the parents' opinions regarding their child's problems. This is an opportunity to gather background information from the parents, including the history of the child's problems, their previous efforts to change his behavior, and sources of stress on the family.

At the end of the meeting, the parents' consent is obtained both for their own and their child's participation (the consent form is reproduced in Appendix 3). Because the child usually has been referred to the program by the court or the Children's Services Division, the parents' permission technically is not required, but going through the process builds rapport with the parents. Because in most cases the long-term goal is to return the child to live with his parents or relatives after the placement, their cooperation is essential at all stages of the program. From the beginning of our involvement, the parents are encouraged to express their opinions and concerns about the treatment program. Finally, the parents are told that a staff therapist will contact them within a week to schedule their first session.

WEEKLY FAMILY THERAPY SESSIONS

The treatment approach used to work with the parents in the Monitor Program is based on the Social Interactional Family Therapy (SIFT) model developed at OSLC during the early 1960s. This model recognizes the pivotal role parents have in socializing their children and focuses on strengthening specific family management skills shown to be related to the development and maintenance of childhood aggression and delinquency. The treatment model focuses on teaching the parents to reinforce their children before attempting to improve their discipline skills. It was noted earlier that one of the most difficult aspects of treatment is asking the parents to change their discipline methods. The therapist is in a better position to work on discipline skills once the parents have successfully implemented an incentive system; this also allows the parents and therapist to establish a collaborative relationship. Numerous outcome studies that have evaluated the effectiveness of this approach (reviewed in Patterson 1985) have shown that the parent-mediated model produces more clinically significant changes in child conduct problems than other treatment models or placebo control treatments. The key components of this treatment model are described in detail in several books (e.g., Patterson 1975; Patterson & Forgatch 1987; Forgatch & Patterson 1989; Patterson et al. 1975) and journal articles (e.g., Patterson & Reid 1973; Patterson, Chamberlain, & Reid 1982). These components are briefly reviewed here.

During the first stage of treatment, parents are taught to systematically identify and observe the child's problem and prosocial behaviors in the home. Then the parents learn how to increase and strengthen the child's level of prosocial responding; the parents systematically reinforce the child for complying with requests, completing chores, and attempting to use good relationship skills such as getting along with siblings and interacting positively with parents (e.g., no arguing, whining, or swearing). In the context of the TFC model, parents are taught to adapt the child's daily point chart to their home setting. Points are given for a variety of prosocial behaviors, such as completing self-care and household chores on time, having a positive attitude (e.g., being pleasant and not pushing the limits), being patient, minding, following established house rules, and being where they are supposed to be with proper supervision. The home point charts start out simple, and then are expanded as the parents become more proficient at using the system. An example of a home point chart is provided in Table 4.2.

Once the parents have learned to reinforce their child and feel comfortable using the daily point chart to encourage positive behaviors, they begin to work on their discipline skills. The parents are taught to use nonviolent methods to give corrective feedback and provide consequences for the child's misbehavior or

Table 4.2
Example of a Home Point Chart

Behavior	Description	Deadline	Points
Arguing about points	Arguing about points taken away will cost you 5 points for each statement		
Cooperation/ Doing Chores	Doing what is asked of you without arguing or talking back and getting chores done in a reasonable amount of time		10
Attitude/maturity	Being pleasant, responsible, and hearing *no* without arguing	(morning) (afternoon)	25 25
Consideration	Showing respect for other members of the family by having a pleasant attitude toward them		10
Volunteering	Seeing what needs to be done and doing it without being asked		10
TOTAL			80
The points you earn during home visits will be exchanged for Level 2 points and privileges when you return.			

rule violations. Effective discipline involves the consistent use of natural or negative consequences. In the TFC model, parents are instructed to take away points as a negative consequence for prespecified target behaviors such as arguing, noncompliance, and physical or verbal aggression; this is a dramatic change for parents who have previously responded to misbehavior by yelling, threatening, or ignoring problems.

The therapist also teaches the parents how to handle discipline episodes without getting angry at the child. Most of these parents find it difficult to control their negative emotions during discipline confrontations. In some families, discipline has consisted entirely of physical control methods. It was noted in Chapter 1 that one-half of the boys and one-third of the girls who have participated in the Monitor Program have been documented victims of physical abuse. Although in most cases the abusing parent is no longer living with the family, violence has become an accepted method for controlling children's behavior.

In the family therapy sessions, the parents learn how to reduce the intensity of discipline confrontations. Several methods are used: disengaging from arguments with the child, delivering consequences in a neutral or even sympathetic manner, and preventing the child's misbehavior from escalating by identifying early signs of problem behavior and immediately taking away a few points to interrupt the chain of behavior. Parents who report that it is difficult for them to control their anger toward the child are taught to recognize when they are angry and take a five-minute break or count to ten to calm down before confronting the child. Most parents assume it is necessary to do something right away, but it is better for them to wait if they are not able to control their anger. In some cases, the therapist will tell the parents to call if they have such an incident.

The family therapists working with adolescents in the Monitor Program are available on-call for parents throughout the treatment. When parents model skills for anger control, it helps the child learn how to control his anger as well.

The family configuration has implications for the way discipline is used. In two-parent families, parents often disagree about the methods that should be used for discipline and when to use them. One parent may view the other as too harsh or lenient; this dynamic is frequently encountered in stepfamilies. In single-parent families, the parent tends to be too lenient and unable or unwilling to set limits for the child. An inordinate number of outside stressors impinging on the family and parental guilt may contribute to this pattern.

Using Role-Playing Exercises in Treatment

Throughout the treatment process, the therapist uses role-playing exercises to help parents learn how to implement the various techniques being taught. These exercises allow parents to practice key interactions and receive feedback on their performance. Going through a series of practice trials on administering discipline or reinforcement to their child helps parents become more skilled and confident in real-life situations. It also allows the therapist to identify areas that are particularly difficult for parents and provides an opportunity to coach them on communicating more effectively.

One of the problems with using role-playing in family treatment is that the parents are often shy or defensive when they are asked to participate. The therapist should recognize this and try to make the role-playing situation as nonthreatening as possible. One technique that was developed by the therapists at OSLC is the "Wrong Way – Right Way" method. Here the therapist sets it up so the parent is instructed to do it wrong first. For example, if the purpose is to have the parent give a reward and praise to the child in a positive and enthusiastic way, the instructions would be something like the following:

> Now pretend I'm your son and I've cleaned up the kitchen just like you asked me to. You're going to tell me that I've done a good job and give me an extra 2 points. Let's assume you're really not that pleased because it's the first time I've cleaned the kitchen all week. I've finally done it right. Also, let's say that you've had a stressful day, you have lots of financial worries, and you're feeling pretty down. Now, act as depressed as possible, and tell me that you appreciate my efforts, and that you're giving me extra points.

The therapist then reinforces the parent for doing a good job of acting depressed, uninterested, angry, or sarcastic. The specific behaviors the parent used to convey the negative message are praised. For example, the therapist might say:

> That was great! You used a sad tone of voice, and you didn't make eye contact at all. Even though you said, "Good job," it didn't sound like you meant it. You seemed preoccupied and didn't even look at what I had done in the kitchen. Also you talked very softly and had almost no inflection in your voice. That was great. The message I got was that you were either unimpressed or preoccupied with something else.

This method allows the therapist to give parents specific feedback on their behavior without being critical of their performance. In fact, the therapist can acknowledge the parent's inability to be reinforcing. Doing it the wrong way may actually be cathartic for some parents. It is an opportunity for the therapist to acknowledge and support how the parents are feeling and to help them improve the way they interact with their child during stressful situations. For example, the therapist could acknowledge that in some situations it is natural for parents to want to let their child know they are upset or angry, but expressing their anger will interfere with their ability to deal with the child's misbehavior. The goal is to help the child change.

Next, the therapist has the parents role-play the right way. In the above example, the parent would be instructed to tell the child that he or she has earned extra points in a positive, supportive way. The therapist again provides feedback to the parents on their performance. It is important to begin by commenting on something the parents have done well before giving corrective feedback. If the parents seem to have problems controlling their negative feelings during the role-playing exercise, the therapist should review some of the methods discussed earlier.

Problems are bound to arise during discipline confrontations at home. Another useful technique is to reenact the parents' unsuccessful attempts to use discipline (i.e., blowups). This gives parents a chance to identify where they went wrong and learn better ways to handle similar situations in the future. Even small gains made by the parents should be reinforced. In this way, the parents gradually improve their skills as the treatment progresses.

Troubleshooting and Solving Problems

The final set of skills taught to parents are communication, negotiation, and problem-solving strategies. These skills are described in detail in *Parents and Adolescents Living Together*, Part 2: *Family Problem Solving* (Forgatch & Patterson 1989). In the TFC model, this phase of treatment is conducted primarily in joint sessions that are attended by the parents, their teenager, and in many cases the other siblings who are living at home. The child's therapist and the parents' therapist are both present at the joint sessions. Typically, joint sessions are held during the last three months of the child's placement in the TFC program.

During the joint sessions, the parents' therapist takes the lead in setting up the agenda and directing the session. The child's therapist gives the child support and acts as his coach. The two therapists meet before the sessions to set specific behavioral goals and plan the agenda. It is often helpful to have separate meetings for the first 20 minutes of the session between the child and his therapist and the parents and their therapist. During this time, the therapists can prepare their respective clients for what will happen in the joint session. The goal is to set the parents and child up for success, to anticipate problems that may come up in the joint session and come up with ways to handle them, and to motivate the family members to practice new ways of interacting.

CASE EXAMPLE: JOHN LEARNS TO TALK TO HIS MOTHER

At the age of 17, John's police record included several burglaries and a series of criminal mischief charges arising out of activities with his peers. He was tall, blond, and good-looking. He had a charming smile and convincing manner. John also had a quick temper and an angry style of interacting with people who got in his way. He used a lot of forceful negative talk and had a history of getting into physical fights at school. John's mother and stepfather felt that neither John nor the family had any real problems. They thought John was just going through a phase and seemed confident he would soon grow out of it.

John's mother was an alcoholic who had stopped drinking four years earlier. Before that, members of her family considered her to be irresponsible and unreliable. During the joint sessions, it became apparent that John did many things to undermine his mother's attempts to exercise parental authority. Although there was clearly a lot of affection between them, John regularly interrupted her, talked over her, and disagreed with her before she had a chance to make her point or express herself. The mother was timid and tentative when talking to her son. By contrast, John interacted appropriately with his stepfather.

The therapists wanted to help the mother become more forceful and teach John to be more respectful when his mother spoke. Several role-playing exercises were used during the joint sessions to accomplish these goals. For example, the mother was given the assignment of saying no to John three times during the session. To make it less threatening, she was given the option of saying no to unimportant or silly things that John would not do anyway (e.g., "Don't sing while we're talking"). John's therapist edited together several sections of videotape of family sessions in which John used appropriate communication skills such as waiting for the other person to finish before speaking. John watched the edited tape with his therapist, and he was reinforced for using positive communication strategies. Then John was told that he could earn points during the sessions for paraphrasing what his mother said before reacting. Several other related strategies were used with John. His assignment for one session was to teach his sister to disagree with their mother in a nonangry, nonconfrontational way. After six weeks of this type of direct training, the verbal performance of both mother and son gradually improved. The focus on current events allowed unresolved issues from the past, such as whether John had problems or his mother had let him down, became secondary. Working on ongoing interactions strengthened the functional relationship between them.

In this case, practicing a variety of skills during the treatment session seemed to be a better strategy than just talking about what needed to be changed. The sessions allowed family members to experience new or underused ways of interacting that could be generalized to out-of-session situations.

ACTIONS AND REACTIONS

As parents try to change the way they deal with their child, the child might intensify his efforts to resist parental control. It is helpful to warn parents in advance that this may happen and emphasize that their reaction at this point can be pivotal. Consistency and follow-through are stressed. Typically, the program therapist and family therapist work together to help the parents get through these difficult times. The parents are encouraged to call if they experience problems during the child's home visits, particularly if his problem behavior escalates. After assessing the situation, the case manager might decide to terminate the child's home visit early. It is easier for parents to follow through with rules and consequences when this option is available to them. Knowing that home visits can end early helps the child maintain self-control and accept his parents' direction.

Information about the problems encountered by family members during treatment sessions or home visits is used to refine and redirect the case plan throughout the course of treatment. The parents are encouraged to discuss aspects of the program or suggestions offered by the therapists that did not work for them. The most difficult families to treat are those in which the parents withhold information or report that everything is fine and that there are no problems. As suggested by Patterson, it is the struggle between the parent and therapist that provides the impetus for making progress in this approach to family treatment.

SUMMARY

As family therapy progresses, the parents and the therapist must come to an understanding about effective methods for supporting, supervising, and disciplining the program adolescent within family, school, and community settings. This is essential for a successful outcome. Typically, the parents are somewhat reticent at first, and they gradually become active, cooperative members of the treatment team as they gain trust and confidence in the therapist and the program. The challenge of attempting to change long-standing family problems is considerable for parents, adolescents, and therapists alike.

The steps taken to prepare the family members for the adolescent's eventual return home probably have the most influence on long-term case outcome. Parents may be optimistic about the positive changes their child has made during the TFC placement. Ultimately, however, case outcome depends upon whether the child can return home and continue to be successful in the family and community. To achieve long-term success, parents have to be convinced that they must become experts at providing their child with close supervision, effective discipline, and appropriate encouragement. In addition to convincing parents about the importance of these factors, we have found that it is helpful for the program to provide them with support and back-up resources during the child's transition from foster care to home.

5

INDIVIDUAL THERAPY FOR THE CHILD

In the context of the overall program, the adolescent's therapist serves as an advocate and coach. The therapist is a source of steady support and encouragement throughout the child's stay in the program and during aftercare. The therapist works with the youth to identify problem areas and designs interventions to help the child improve his skills in those areas. The overarching goal of individual therapy is to facilitate the child's adjustment in the foster home and at school.

The child and therapist first meet when the child is brought to OSLC immediately prior to placement in the foster home. The purpose of the meeting is to introduce the teenager to the treatment foster parents and the program therapist, review the child's point chart, and explain how the program works. This chapter describes the role of the therapist and the types of interventions used.

After being introduced by the case manager, the therapist and child have a brief meeting before he goes home with the treatment foster parents for the first time. The therapist explains that he or she will be the teenager's advocate and will give the adolescent support and guidance to ensure his success in the program. The child is told that they will usually meet weekly but that they can meet more often if the child requests it. The therapist tells the adolescent that their next meeting will be in three days. After three days of placement, an acceptance meeting is held, at which time the youth is officially welcomed into the program. In the meantime, the child is encouraged to contact the therapist if any problems come up during the first three days that need to be discussed. The teenager is given the telephone numbers for the therapist's office and home.

THE ACCEPTANCE MEETING

The acceptance meeting takes place three days later. It is attended by the case manager, one or both of the foster parents, the child, and the child's therapist. The purpose of the meeting is threefold: (1) to review the adolescent's initial adjustment in the foster home from both his perspective and that of the foster parents; (2) to help the teenager determine the personal goals he would like to accomplish during the placement time; and (3) to officially accept the youth into the program.

During the first half of the session, the therapist meets with the child individually and asks him to identify two or three main goals he will work toward while he is in the program. The child usually describes goals in general terms such as "Staying out of trouble with the law," "Going to school," "Passing my classes," or "Getting along better with my family." The therapist offers support and helps the teenager formulate goals that are both specific and attainable. The therapist asks how things are going at the foster home and discusses any problems the child may be experiencing. Then the therapist reviews how often they will meet, tells the youth that he or she will call occasionally to find out how things are going, and invites the child to call when he is upset or discouraged or for any other reason. Finally, the teenager is reminded that the therapist's role is to provide help and support.

Next, the child and therapist attend a joint meeting with the case manager and foster parent(s). The case manager begins by asking the foster parents how things have been going so far. This is an ideal time for the foster parents to make positive comments about the adolescent. They should acknowledge that he is earning points for good behavior and getting along with other family members. They should also confirm that they generally like the foster child. The case manager then asks the teenager to describe how he views the situation and has him explain the personal goals that he will work on during placement. The therapist helps the youth articulate these goals if he is shy or withdrawn.

Next, the therapist expresses his or her opinion. The therapist usually indicates that although he or she has just met the child, it appears the child will do well in the program. The therapist should refer to some specific aspect of the interactions he or she has had with the adolescent so far to support this statement. For example, the therapist might say:

> I think Shawn will do very well in the program. He does a good job of talking about the problems he is facing, and this is the first step toward solving them. Also, I think that when he makes mistakes, he will be able to handle the consequences the program lays down.

The case manager then asks the child to predict which part of the program will be most difficult to handle. The adolescent is reinforced for identifying a potential problem area, and he is assured that the therapist will be there to help deal with any problems that come up during the course of the placement.

The case manager asks the foster parents how the child has reacted to losing points. At the time of the acceptance meeting (which is three days into the placement) the foster parents may not have taken any points away from him. In this situation, the case manager instructs the foster parents to do so within the next 24 hours. The case manager says something like this:

> I know things have been going well, and it's hard to know what to take points away for, but I want Shawn to experience what it's like to lose a point or two before a real problem comes up. It's hard to lose points for the first time and have to deal with a problem, too. We want him to get used to losing points so it's not a big deal. Even if you have to be incredibly picky or even make something up, take a point or two away before tomorrow at this time. Do you think you can handle that, Shawn?

This "practice run" desensitizes the adolescent to losing a few points for small infractions and eases the foster parents' guilt about being overcritical of him. The case manager ends the meeting with a positive statement about the child's good start. The youth is then officially accepted into the program, and he is given a special T-shirt with his name or a picture of something he enjoys on it (e.g., a sports activity, hobby, or aspiration).

THE INITIAL PHASE OF TREATMENT

Building a Support Base

The therapist usually spends the first two or three weekly treatment sessions getting acquainted with the child's likes, interests, future aspirations, and fantasies. The teenager also is asked to describe his strengths. Starting treatment this way has many advantages. Assessing the adolescent's positive qualities and skills is a nonthreatening way for the therapist to establish a relationship with him. In general, the treatment focuses on the here and now, and it is often helpful to make the sessions activity oriented (e.g., going for short walks, playing a game for part of the session, buying the child a snack). By "doing" in addition to talking, the therapist can observe the child's skills while he is interacting with others in a variety of situations. The therapist uses the information collected during this phase to adapt subsequent interventions to fit the needs of the youth and to reinforce his positive self-perceptions.

It is relatively common for TFC children to present themselves as shy, withdrawn, or hostile during the initial therapy sessions. These children often respond to the therapist's questions with one-word answers. When this happens, the therapist can shift the discussion to topics that are trivial and nonpersonal, such as sports, music, hobbies, or movies and television programs the youngster enjoys. The therapist might tell the adolescent about his or her own hobbies and interests or talk about hypothetical situations. The use of humor is encouraged. This approach usually helps the teenager relax. During the beginning stages of treatment, the therapist should not confront the adolescent or try to interpret his resistance to participating in treatment. We have found it is more effective to ignore the youth's resistance and focus instead on building a relationship between the therapist and the child.

During the "getting to know you" stage of treatment, the therapist should look for opportunities to praise the child for specific skills and try to identify personal resources that will help him succeed in the program. Gradually, the therapist can begin to talk about areas that may be difficult for the teenager. As treatment progresses, these concerns and problems can be selected as targets for specific interventions designed to increase the child's competencies. Our experience with antisocial youths suggests it is important to avoid talking about problems right away; these children will either deny or minimize problems, or readily "cop" to problems in an attempt to get the therapist off their back. This is especially true for youngsters who have previously been in therapy. They are skilled at giving the therapist the response they think the therapist wants.

From Advocacy to Empowerment

Throughout treatment, the child is given the message that the therapist is on his side and that the goal is to help him learn to solve problems and negotiate for changes in the program. Inevitably, the youth begins to experience problems in at least one of the major settings in which he must interact with others (e.g., at home, at school, in the community). Each incident is viewed as an opportunity to learn more about the child's behavioral deficits and excesses and help the child develop the skill or self-control necessary to behave more appropriately. This means the therapist should encourage the adolescent to talk about the problem situation in terms of its behavioral characteristics, antecedents, and the feelings the adolescent had before or during the event that contributed to his acting out. The therapist works with the child to come up with several alternatives to handle the distressing situation. Often, a youth who has had an explosive outburst will be reluctant or unwilling to discuss the details of the event. In these situations, we have found that it is helpful to reenact the event (this technique is described later in the chapter).

If the teenager thinks a certain program consequence is unfair, the therapist prompts him to negotiate for changes in consequences for similar situations that may come up in the *future*. The consequences for a current infraction are not negotiable, because it is not therapeutic to alter consequences during the course of a discipline event; this teaches the adolescent that he can avoid consequences by arguing about them.

In negotiating consequences or other changes in the child's daily program, the therapist and child work through the following three steps: (1) Clearly state what needs to be changed, (2) identify the changes the child is willing to make to facilitate the situation, and (3) determine how the child's behavior will be tracked to evaluate whether the change has had a positive or at least neutral effect on his adjustment and daily performance. The therapist then helps the youth practice the first two steps in a role-playing exercise. The therapist assumes the role of case manager, and the adolescent presents his request for change. The therapist provides reinforcement and corrective feedback after each attempt. The role-playing should be repeated several times until the child's presentation improves.

Next, a meeting is arranged with the case manager, therapist, and adolescent. The therapist usually contacts the case manager before the meeting to discuss the change the teenager will be requesting. That way, if the case manager needs more information before the change can be approved (e.g., it may be necessary to check with the foster parents or school personnel), these details can be taken care of prior to meeting with the child. During the meeting, the therapist supports the child and facilitates the negotiation process as he makes his request for a change in the program. The case manager tries to grant the child's request, if it is appropriate, or compromise with the child by granting at least part of the change that has been requested. The purpose of this process is to teach the youth how to make constructive changes through negotiation and compromise.

Case Coordination and Targeting Behaviors for Change

The adolescent's therapist works with the case manager and foster parents to identify the adolescent's specific behavior problems and skill deficits and develops interventions to correct them. Ideally, interventions should be simultaneously implemented in more than one setting (e.g., at home, in therapy sessions, and at school). This requires careful coordination among members of the teenager's treatment team.

For example, the child may have a problem in the foster home such as hitting or yelling at a younger child. In this situation, the therapist asks the adolescent to describe what the younger child did to provoke his inappropriate response. The discussion focuses on the specific events that happened before and during the confrontation. Then the therapist works with the youth to generate a list of alternative responses that could have been used in the same type of situation. It is helpful to include several frivolous or humorous options. Next, the child practices using one or two of the alternatives by having the therapist role-play the part of a younger child whose behavior is irritating. As a follow-up assignment, the therapist asks the child to practice at least one alternative to hitting and yelling every day during the next week; the child is instructed to write down the details of the situation and how he responded. The child should be offered a small incentive or reward for his efforts to carry out the assignment; the criterion for the reward should be reasonable (i.e., not require a perfect performance), for example, completing the assignment on five out of the next seven days.

The therapist informs the case manager

about the assignment, and the case manager works with the foster parents to design a corresponding intervention at home. For instance, revising the child's point chart to include points that can be earned on a daily basis for showing patience with the younger child. In this way, the program youth receives support and reinforcement for his attempts to change the problem behavior from both the therapist and the foster parents simultaneously. Interventions are coordinated with the school setting as well (details are provided in Chapter 7). We find that helping the child change well-entrenched problem behavior patterns requires coordinated interventions conducted in multiple settings. The adolescent's individual therapist is a key player in developing, initiating, coordinating, and following through with these interventions.

THE REENACTMENT TECHNIQUE

In some instances, the child will resist the therapist's attempts to review a problem situation. The child may deny that the problem occurred at all, minimize it, or place the blame on others. This dynamic often arises in the context of a serious or volatile situation. This makes it difficult or impossible for the therapist to proceed to the problem-solving stage (i.e., making a list of alternative options) with the adolescent. To overcome this problem, we have developed a reenactment technique. The following case example illustrates how this technique is used.

Case Example: Troy Loses His Shorts

Troy, a 14-year-old boy, had been suspended from school for throwing a tantrum in the main office at school. When his therapist attempted to debrief the situation with him and think of other possible options, Troy's response was, "I didn't do anything. I don't remember what happened. It was no big deal." The therapist replied, "That's too bad, because if you can't recall what happened, there is no way for us to figure out how you could have handled the situation differently. I'll have to think about how to help you on this one." After having a conference with the case manager, it was decided that the best approach would be to use the reenactment technique. The plan involved contacting the teacher who had been present during the outburst and inviting her to come to the next treatment session.

The subsequent session was attended by the case manager, teacher (Mrs. James), therapist, and child. The case manager began by introducing the problem:

Case manager: Troy had a problem in school yesterday. He's having a hard time remembering exactly what happened, so I thought it would be a good idea to run through the situation again. Then we can help him figure out what else he could have done in that situation. We are making a videotape of this discussion so he and his therapist can watch it later and decide what his options were in that situation. Mrs. James, could you briefly describe what happened? Pretend you were making a movie of the scene. How did it look? What were you and Troy doing that led to the blowup?

Mrs. James: Well, Troy didn't have his gym shorts. This meant he couldn't participate in gym class, so I asked him to write 20 sentences as a consequence. He argued with me about this, so I added 10 more sentences. Then he refused to do them. I told him that if he didn't get started on the sentences right away, he would have to stay after school to do them. At that point, he became very upset and said he wanted to call his mother. We walked down to the office to make the call.

After he talked to his mother for a minute or two, he threw the phone at me, swore loudly, hit the wall, and stormed out of the office. The principal came out and said Troy was suspended for two days.

Case manager: (turning to Troy) Okay, let's run through the scene from the time you went to the office to make the call. I'll play your mother, Troy. What did she say to you on the telephone?

Troy: (avoiding eye contact) She said I should do the sentences. But I told her it wasn't fair — someone stole my shorts!

Case manager: What did your mom say then?

Troy: She said I should write the sentences anyway, and she promised to get me some new shorts later.

Case manager: Good, let's run through the scene again. This time we'll act it out. I'll play Troy's mom. Mrs. James will play herself. Troy can you play yourself?

Troy agreed to play himself. However, it is fairly common for children to refuse to cooperate at this stage. Had he refused, the case manager would have said, "That's okay, you can watch. I understand it's difficult for you to do this. Just watch, and don't say anything. If you feel upset or want to talk about something you can write a note to your therapist on this pad. Now, I would like the two of you (the child and the therapist) to sit over there, and we'll act out the situation." If the child refuses to participate, he or she is asked to simply observe the reenactment.

As the scene was reenacted, Troy was much more subdued than he had been in the real situation. For example, he handed the telephone to Mrs. James rather than throwing it as he had the day before, and he said he could not remember the swear words that he had used. Mrs. James wrote them down for him, and the scene was replayed again. This time Troy used all the words he had used the day before, but his tone of voice was soft and he still handed the telephone to Mrs. James. The therapist praised Troy for trying, but the case manager said they had to run through the scene again because they had not gotten it right yet. At this point Troy said, "It's just that I feel so stupid. At the time it seemed all right, but now I don't want to yell the swear words. It's embarrassing. Besides, I'm afraid I'll hurt you (to Mrs. James) with the telephone." Mrs. James said, "I'm ready for it this time. Try doing it like this," then she threw the telephone receiver at him.

The scene was reenacted again. This time Mrs. James said that it was close to what had happened the day before. Both Troy and Mrs. James were thanked for their participation. Troy was told that he had acted maturely, and that it must have been difficult for him to replay the scene so many times. The videotape of the session was sent home with Troy, and he was given the assignment of watching it at least once before his therapy session the next day. Later that day, Troy's therapist called to ask how he was doing. Armed with the videotape, the therapist and Troy worked on generating a list of alternative responses Troy could use in similar situations.

It is important when conducting reenactments to take a sympathetic stance toward the child. Even if the youth just observes the reenactment, it is a difficult and emotional experience for him or her. The goal is not to punish the child but to counteract the child's efforts to deny or minimize what happened or ignore the effects of his or her problem behavior. We have used this type of role-playing in a variety of situations. For example: A boy refused to leave the classroom and the police were eventually called; a boy refused to do a chore, had a temper tantrum, and threw a glass across the room; a boy threw a desk at his teacher; a girl ripped a shrub out of the foster parent's front lawn when she was told she could not go out.

TEACHING SOCIAL AND RELATIONAL SKILLS

The individual sessions provide opportunities for the therapist to help the child improve his social and relationship skills and to teach new ones. The first step for the therapist is to identify specific target areas for intervention. Potential targets are selected based on observations of the child or information provided by the case manager, foster parents, or other significant adults with whom the child has contact (e.g., teachers). The recommended approach is to start simple and work on more complex skills as therapy progresses. The process of identification and targeting continues throughout treatment.

The specific skill-training exercises or practices can be presented to the child as a step toward one of the goals he has previously identified (e.g., making friends, getting along better with teachers). In addition to using structured methods such as role-playing or practice exercises, shaping and modeling are used to encourage behaviors that are viewed as appropriate and adaptive. To teach the teenager alternatives to problem behavior, the therapist also may choose to include contracts and consequences.

Modeling Problem-Solving Skills

We have found that it is useful to begin working with the child on an issue or topic he is not personally involved in so he can focus on the problem-solving process without becoming defensive. For example, the therapist can talk about how he or she handled a difficult situation or ask for the child's advice on what the therapist or a hypothetical child should do in a particular situation. This technique is used to teach the adolescent to brainstorm several possible solutions and discuss their advantages and disadvantages. The therapist reinforces the child as often as possible during the sessions, emphasizing the skills he used successfully and drawing parallels to skills he used during the past week. The goal is to build the teenager's confidence in his ability to identify potential problems, generate possible solutions, and practice those solutions in real-life situations.

Teaching Alternatives to Problem Behaviors

In many cases, the child will exhibit problem behaviors during treatment sessions such as being sullen, surly, inattentive, or argumentative. In joint sessions with the child and his parents, family members often make derogatory remarks to one another or interrupt and talk over another person. Once these problems are observed, the therapist can design an intervention to change them. The following are some examples of similar in-session interventions.

Decreasing "Zapping" Among Family Members

Rude remarks and put-downs are often interspersed in the interactions among family members during the treatment sessions. Sometimes the unpleasant responses are subtle, and at other times they are blunt and forceful. Although it may be important to "clear the air" on occasion, the persistent exchange of negative remarks is rarely a productive use of session time. Once it starts, it can be difficult to stop, because everyone wants to have the last word. In this situation, family members need to learn techniques they can use to keep the negative exchanges from escalating. Our approach is to label negative remarks as "zaps" and give several examples of the zaps family members have used during the session.

The therapist explains that he or she is concerned that the sessions have not been as productive or as pleasant as they should be due to the conflict among family members. Then the therapist introduces the idea of tracking every time someone makes a negative remark, or zap. This is an effective way to suppress negative interactions. Families are generally receptive to the intervention if it is presented in a supportive, nonblaming way. The therapist writes everyone's name on a blackboard, therapist included. Every time a zap occurs, the therapist simply makes a mark on the board next to the offender's name. If the therapist does not want to interrupt the ongoing flow of interaction, it is not necessary to label the zap or comment on it. When one family member is doing all the zapping, the therapist may want to purposely use a mild zap to diffuse the blame.

This technique teaches family members to be more aware of their negative interchanges. It also gives them a way to deal with zaps outside the therapy sessions. As a further step, the therapist can ask the family to practice at home by having one family member track zaps during the next family meeting, with the understanding that the family meeting will be ended if more than a certain number of zaps occur.

A similar technique can be used to work on the problem of interrupting and talking over. The steps are as follows:

1. The therapist identifies the problem behavior and defines it.

2. The therapist provides a brief rationale to the family members for decreasing the behavior.

3. The therapist explains that he or she intends to track the occurrence of the problem behavior during the session.

4. The therapist lists the names of everyone participating in the session, and tracks each occurrence of the problem by making a mark next to the appropriate person's name.

5. (Optional) The therapist sets a limit on the number of occurrences allowed before the session will be ended.

Using Immediate Rewards and Sanctions

In some cases, the child's social skills are poor or inappropriate. In addition to discussing better ways to interact with others, therapy sessions can be used to practice new ways of relating. In these instances, the adolescent should be immediately reinforced for attempting to improve a skill or learn a new one. Alternately, it is instructive to provide a small consequence when the child exhibits an inappropriate behavior. Tokens that are later traded for a prize and treats can be given or taken away contingent on the child's performance. The following case example illustrates the use of this technique.

CASE EXAMPLE: THE BOY WITH THE INCREDIBLE BRAIN

Larry had been told throughout his childhood that he was gifted. Both he and his mother were convinced it was difficult for normal people to relate to him because of his superior intelligence. Larry had been diagnosed by a court-appointed psychologist as having Attention Deficit Disorder with Hyperactivity. He had a history of arguing with teachers and peers in school and was placed in a classroom for emotionally disturbed teenagers.

Larry had been referred to the TFC program after an incident at home in which he chased his sister through the house with a butcher knife and then stuck it in the bathroom door when she slammed it in his face. This incident was the culmination of many years of increasingly violent arguments between family members. The arguments would start out as verbal disagreements and eventually escalate into physical confrontations. At the time of referral, Larry was 13 years old, and he was getting too big for his mother to handle physically. Another problem was that Larry had no friends his age. He was routinely rejected by his peers and had been kicked out of the Boy Scouts and several school sports teams.

During the first session, the therapist noticed several problems with Larry's interactional skills. He did not take turns in conversation; he would take over the conversation and not let anyone else talk. Larry engaged in long monologues and interrupted and talked over the therapist when he tried to join in. In addition, Larry did not make appropriate eye contact with the person to whom he was speaking; he gazed off to the side. The therapist assumed that this strategy was functional for Larry because it allowed him to ignore the other person's cues that he or she had something to say.

During the first two sessions, the therapist concentrated on learning about Larry's interests and his view of himself in relation to others. Larry felt that because of his high intelligence, he was often misunderstood. He thought that if other people would listen to him more carefully, everything would be fine. During the fifth session, the therapist told Larry that he had been thinking about what Larry had been saying about people not listening to him. The therapist said he thought he knew what the problem was: Larry was very bright, but he did not know how to get his points across effectively. Then he told Larry that they were going to work on this in the sessions by practicing some strategies Larry could use to make his message more powerful. This appealed to Larry because it validated his original statement that people misunderstood him, and it gave him something to try.

As a starting point, the therapist targeted two skills he wanted to practice with Larry; taking turns and making good eye contact. The therapist offered support by saying that it was very difficult to practice new ways of communicating but that they were going to do some role-playing to make it easier. During the practice session, Larry would earn a paper clip (our version of tokens) each time he gave the therapist a turn to talk or looked at the therapist's face. Interrupting and talking over would mean that Larry would lose a paper clip. At the end of the session, if Larry had more than a certain number of paper clips, the therapist would buy him an ice cream cone.

Using this method, the therapist was able to work directly with Larry on interaction patterns that were a problem for him. Once Larry was able to improve his turn taking and eye contact, other behaviors, such as listening and paraphrasing were targeted. The foster parents reinforced Larry by giving him points for these new skills at home.

SUMMARY

The child's therapist plays a central role in the treatment process. To be effective, the therapist must strike a balance between being the adolescent's advocate and coordinating the treatment plan with other members of the treatment team. In our program model, the fine points of the therapist's role have evolved through trial and error. In the early days of the program, for example, the case manager often conducted the individual therapy sessions with the child. However, we soon realized that this put the therapist in the awkward position of setting limits or saying no instead of being an advocate for the child. This detracted from the therapist's ability to encourage, support, and empathize with the adolescent.

The therapist must gain the child's trust and

create a therapeutic milieu in which the child feels safe talking about difficult subjects. To help the teenager improve his skills for dealing with adults and peers, the therapist has to understand his point of view and current level of functioning. At the same time, the therapist must work within the auspices of the TFC model as an important member of the child's treatment team. This role involves coordinating the treatment plan with the case manager, foster parents, family therapist, and school personnel to ensure that common goals are addressed throughout the placement. It takes experience to do this job well. For example, novice therapists will often overidentify with the teenager and take the position that the solution to all problems is to have the foster parents or teachers change or decrease their demands. Although situations often develop that warrant some change from adults, the primary goal of the program is to help the child develop skills that enable him to function without creating problems in the community. By the end of treatment, the program should not be making extensive exceptions or special arrangements for the child; otherwise, it is very unlikely he will continue to make progress in aftercare.

In most cases, an experienced therapist can greatly increase the youth's therapeutic progress during the placement period. The therapist can provide a place for the child to talk about his problems, give the treatment team insights into his struggles, and sympathize with his point of view without undermining the goals of the program. When properly conducted, the therapy sessions are a forum for the child to celebrate his successes, large and small.

6

CASE MANAGEMENT ONE: WORKING WITH FOSTER PARENTS, BIOLOGICAL PARENTS, AND THERAPISTS

In our Treatment Foster Care model, the case manager is the leader of the treatment team. Case managers typically handle from 5 to 7 cases at a time; 10 cases is the absolute limit. Small caseloads allow case managers to attend to all aspects of each case as necessary on a daily basis. Case managers must have clinical training and experience, be familiar with the program model and the client population targeted by the TFC program, and be accustomed to working with foster parents. Case managers need to be effective communicators who can deal with professionals from a variety of disciplines as well as with the client population being served. Usually, our case managers are therapists who have worked with the program for at least one year and are well acquainted with the working systems and goals of the program. The ability of the case manager to coordinate the various roles of treatment team members is the key to a successful outcome for program youths and their families.

The case manager coordinates and supervises the implementation of the child's treatment plan. The case manager works with all members of the child's treatment team, including the foster parents, the child's therapist, the biological family's therapist, the parole or probation officer, and school personnel. In our model, the foster parents and both therapists (the child's and the biological family's) are employed by the program; the probation or parole worker is an employee of the state Children's Services Division. The case manager's task is a complex one. He or she is responsible for balancing the agendas of all team members to provide the adolescent with a sensible, integrated treatment plan. At the same time, the case manager is the "end of the line" when decisions — sometimes unpopular — need to made about program changes, negative consequences, and other essential matters. It is important to establish effective mechanisms for frequent communication between the case manager and other members of the treatment team. Figure 6.1 depicts the central role of the case manager in coordinating program services for the participating child, his or her biological family, and the foster parents.

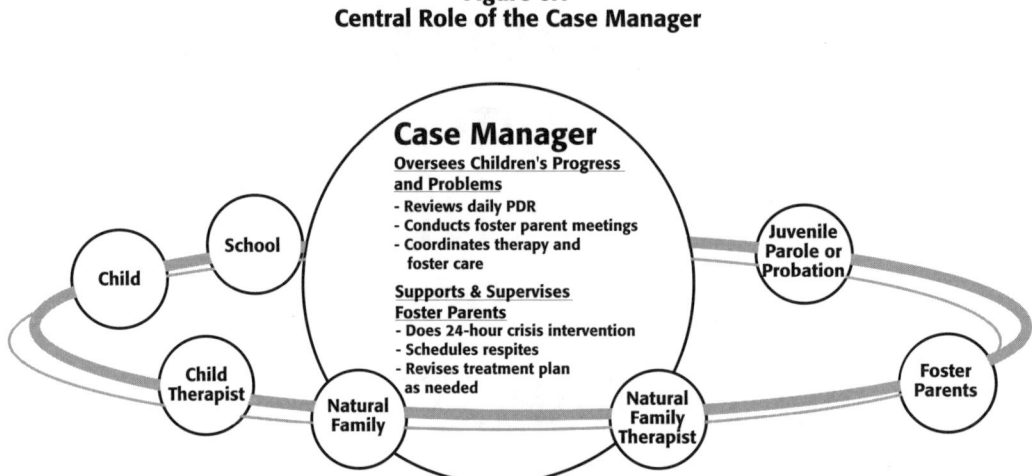

**Figure 6.1
Central Role of the Case Manager**

Communication with Foster Parents

In our model, the case manager contacts each foster parent by telephone daily to collect specific information on the child's progress and problems during the past 24 hours. These telephone data are used to monitor the child's adjustment throughout the placement (see Chapter 10 for a description of the Parent Daily Report checklist used for this purpose). The telephone call also is an opportunity for the case manager to give foster parents support and suggestions.

Weekly group meetings are held with all the program foster parents and the case managers. Usually this meeting includes five to seven sets of foster parents and their associated case managers who conduct a discussion and do planning for each case. The focus of this meeting is on the child's adjustment in the foster home and at school during the past week. The foster parents report on the child's progress and problems, and the point system may be revised if necessary. The case manager shares relevant information with the foster parents about the therapy being implemented with the child's biological family and individually with the child. This meeting also is an opportunity to check with the foster parents to make sure the times that have been tentatively scheduled for the next series of therapy appointments and home visits are convenient for them. The schedule of the foster parents' family is carefully considered in setting up these activities. Therapy sessions should cause as little disruption as possible to the daily routines of the foster family. For example, because we require the foster parents to provide transportation for the child to and from therapy appointments, the case manager makes sure the sessions do not occur at dinnertime or at other times that are inconvenient for the foster parents.

Communication with Therapists

It was mentioned earlier that two separate therapists are assigned to each case: the family's therapist and the child's individual therapist (see Chapters 4 and 5). The case manager must maintain ongoing communication with both therapists to integrate their input into the treatment plan. A weekly clinical meeting is held for this purpose, during which the case manager and therapists discuss each case. Also, the therapists contact the case manager by telephone or in person as needed to exchange information between regularly scheduled weekly meetings.

The weekly clinical meetings are attended by the case managers, the therapists, the program director, and other clinical or psychiatric consultants involved in the program. Typically, five to seven cases are reviewed in two hours. The clinical meetings are used to resolve case issues and to set and review the goals and direction of the case. During these meetings, the case manager presents information about the youth's adjustment in the foster home and at school. Generally, one or two cases receive detailed attention, including a viewing of videotapes of individual and family therapy sessions. The remaining cases are briefly reviewed and discussed. Cases are rotated throughout the month so a comprehensive review is conducted of each case at least once per month. More time is spent on cases that are particularly difficult or complicated and on cases in which there is disagreement or confusion about the treatment plan.

Balancing the Agendas of Foster Parents and Therapists

It is relatively common for the therapist and foster parents to have conflicting goals and agendas. This dynamic was described by Horner, Smith, and Ray (1990) in their article on implementing a Specialized Foster Care program for severely abused children and teenagers in the state of Washington. The authors pointed out that an inherent difference in treatment goals between the therapists and the foster parents and child welfare staff who supervised them caused serious problems in program implementation. In that project, the therapists' goal was to provide treatment for sexual abuse using a Structural Family Therapy approach, while the child welfare workers and foster parents were concerned with providing an environment that was normal and stable. The problems included conflicting philosophies of the therapists and foster parents and scheduling of weekly therapy sessions that interfered with after-school activities and homework time or that interrupted the foster parents' dinner hour and other family activities. It was also noted that the foster parents frequently failed to come in for their therapy appointments. The therapists in that project regarded the foster parents as a target for intervention rather than as a treatment resource. The different agendas interfered with the coordination of two key components of the services delivered to the child — therapy and therapeutic foster care.

In our model, the case manager is responsible for integrating input from therapists and foster parents into the treatment plan. A skilled case manager should have the ability to reframe that input, if necessary. In addition, the case manager may have to translate the therapist's suggestions to make them more acceptable to the foster parents. At times, it is necessary to remind the therapist about the everyday concerns of the foster family. The goal is to create an environment in which the therapy system and the foster parent system will work in concert and to engender a sense of mutual respect between the therapists and foster parents.

Another important aspect of the case manager's role is to help foster parents implement specific targets for behavior change suggested by therapists and clinical consultants into the child's daily point program. For example, the therapist might suggest that a child who has a problem with angry outbursts should go to his room or step outside to take a brief "time out" when he feels himself becoming angry. Without intervention from the case manager, the foster parents might assume that the adolescent should not be allowed to leave because leaving is a manipulative way to get out of facing the situation. The case manager could reframe this issue by telling the foster parents that the first step is to help the child to disengage from his anger. After he learns to do this, he will be taught the problem-solving skills necessary to deal with difficult situations more effectively; for now, the foster parents should give the teenager points for taking "time outs."

Communication with the Child's Biological or Adoptive Parents

From the first contact, the biological or adoptive parents are encouraged to call the case manager when they have questions or want progress reports on how their child is doing in the program. The case manager should be receptive and sensitive to their concerns about issues such as visitation and the special needs of their child. Parents are given the home telephone numbers of project staff members and are told to call the case manager, not the foster parents, when they are upset about something or have questions. The parents are told that all visits are to be arranged through the case manager, not through the foster parents. The rationale for this policy is that home visits need to be coordinated with both of the therapists involved in the case as well as with the foster parents. It also may be necessary to check with a parole or probation officer before a visit is scheduled.

In our model, the case manager is the intermediary between the foster parents and the youth's biological or adoptive parents. This policy prevents the biological or adoptive parents from having direct contact with the foster parents. In our experience this reduces the occurrence of problems such as jealousy, manipulation, and working at cross-purposes with the treatment plan. Also, we want to be extremely careful not to put the adolescent in the position of taking sides between the foster family and his biological family. Loyalty issues are common for this group of youngsters. If the child's biological parents call the foster parents directly, they are told to contact the case manager. Having a program rule that restricts contact between foster parents and biological parents makes it difficult for the child to manipulate the adults and averts the development of split loyalties. This rule is sometimes softened over the course of the placement if the child is adjusting well and jealousy and manipulation issues are not present or are easily resolved. In a few instances, a supportive relationship has developed between the foster parents and the biological parents.

When the biological or adoptive parents have the child return for a home visit, the case manager makes all necessary arrangements (e.g., transportation, times) with the foster parents. Visits vary in length depending on the child's adjustment and progress in the program. The biological parents are assured that program staff will provide back-up support during the visit. If the adolescent refuses to cooperate with the rules set up before the visit or if other problems arise, program staff are available to pick him up and return him to the foster home.

At first, the foster parents and biological parents meet at the program office to deliver the child to and from the visit, thus avoiding having the biological parents go to the foster home. Once the child is stabilized in the program and family therapy is well under way, it is often appropriate to relax the restriction on contact between foster parents and biological parents. However, in some instances, such as cases in which the parents are antagonistic, extremely needy, or overdemanding, it is necessary to keep the foster parents and biological parents separated throughout the placement period.

The topic of home visits is discussed in the family therapy meetings attended by the family therapist, the biological or adoptive parents, and sometimes the teenager (typically during the last three months of placement). The family therapist prepares family members for the visit, but leaves it up to the case manager to arrange a specific time. The reason for this is that the foster parents' schedule must be considered when selecting visit times. Parents are asked to call the case manager directly to set up the home visit. After the family therapy session, the case manager and therapist make preliminary arrangements, and the case manager is asked to confirm this with the foster parents. Although this procedure may seem cumbersome or complicated, it avoids communication problems and misunderstandings among the program staff, foster parents, therapists, and the child's natural parents.

Developing systems of communication that are clear and impartial is a crucial aspect of the case manager's job. It is important for the case manager to treat individual preferences on both sides with respect. Information can sometimes be distorted or manipulated in exchanges between the natural parents and the placement child. In a typical scenario, the teenager gives his natural parents false information to provoke a negative reaction toward the program. Similarly, the adolescent may misinform his foster parents about events that occurred during a home visit. In either situation, the case manager attempts to clear up any misunderstandings by investigating what was said or what happened. To do this effectively, it is necessary to have established a good relationship with the parties concerned. In many cases, we have targeted giving misinformation or omitting information on the child's point chart.

CASE EXAMPLE: JAY'S PIPE DREAM

When Jay returned from a home visit he reported to his foster parents that he and his mother had gone shopping at a "head shop" where they looked at pipes for smoking dope. When the foster parent questioned him about this, he reported that his mom thought the pipes were "cool" and said she would buy him one when he graduated from the program. Understandably, the foster parent was outraged.

The case manager called Jay's mother and asked how the visit had gone and what she and Jay had done. When the mother mentioned shopping, the case manager asked about going to the head shop. The mother said that Jay had gone into the store by himself and that she had to call him four or five times to get him to come out. She said she had not gone in the store with him and certainly had not offered to buy him a pipe. The case manager told her that Jay would lose points for lying. The case manager then discussed this issue with the family therapist.

Interestingly, even though the mother was using a point chart with Jay during visits, she had not taken any points away for his noncompliance at the head shop (i.e., not leaving when she had asked him to). Because the case manager, family therapist, and foster parent worked together, the information gained from this incident was used as a focus for family therapy. The mother learned from this real-life example she should not cover for Jay or let his noncompliant behavior slide. The family therapist discussed this with the mother and helped her practice taking points away for noncompliance by conducting some role-playing exercises.

The case manager made sure that Jay lost more points for lying than he would have lost for noncompliance.

SUMMARY

In the TFC model, the case manager is the central organizer and leader of the treatment team for the child and his family. To be effective in this role, the case manager must develop collaborative relationships with the foster parents and therapists working on the case and be able to balance the agendas of the various treatment components in a way that serves the best interests of the teenager and his family. Case managers must have the training and experience necessary to be respected as the final authority by the other treatment team members. In addition, the case manager's ability to be supportive and encouraging enhances the commitment of the other treatment team members to the case and the program. Our experience suggests that having a strong, supportive case manager greatly potentiates the power of the TFC model to help the child and his family make significant changes.

7

CASE MANAGEMENT TWO: COORDINATING SERVICES WITH OTHER COMMUNITY AGENCIES

Other community agencies often are involved with a case from the time of initial referral to termination from the program. Creating a good relationship between TFC staff and members of these agencies can greatly facilitate the potential of the program to support the youth's positive adjustment. Unfortunately, "turf wars" are common among agency staff, who may have disparate goals and philosophies.

Given that the TFC program model affects the child's entire social sphere, it is imperative to develop a good working relationship with school personnel so information can be routinely obtained on the adolescent's behavior and academic performance. For mandated cases, the parole or probation officer and the judge have the final say about placement of the teenager and about the use of incarceration. Working at cross-purposes with corrections personnel causes confusion and mixed messages. However, if the child commits a law or parole violation while he is in the program, corrections staff may not agree with the TFC program on what should be done.

This chapter discusses the primary issues involved in working with school personnel, probation or parole staff, and juvenile judges and the methods we have developed for dealing with these issues. Although some situations or conditions are undoubtedly unique to our state and local community, most of the information included here should apply to other programs serving similar populations of youngsters.

SCHOOL LIAISON

Typically, the child is placed in a school that is in the home district of the foster parents. There are some exceptions, such as cases in which the adolescent needs to be enrolled in a school that has a special program (e.g., a self-contained special education classroom or a vocational program), but in most cases the teenager changes schools when he is placed in TFC. Although this is somewhat disruptive, it is better to have the child make a fresh start in a new school than to deal with the severe and long-standing problems that have typically occurred in his home school. Sometimes the foster parents have established a good relationship with their local school when their own children or other foster children were attending classes there. This is a factor to consider when hiring

TFC parents — if they have an antagonistic relationship with the local school, it may jeopardize the program child's chances of success.

Prior to enrolling the adolescent in school, the case manager and TFC parents meet with someone from administration (usually the principal, vice principal, or school counselor) to present an overview of the TFC program and review the teenager's educational needs (an overview of the program is reproduced in Appendix 4). The case manager describes the various ways that the program can offer support to the school. This includes regular monitoring of attendance and homework and crisis intervention (someone from the program will pick up the child when necessary). It is clearly stated that Monitor Program staff will be available to school personnel for additional support, meetings, and consultation as needed. If the TFC parents do not attend this initial meeting, a second meeting is scheduled to give them an opportunity to meet with school personnel and select the classes the youngster will be enrolled in.

The School Card

The school counselor or some other key contact person is asked to review a daily school card for use with the program child. The purpose of the card is to give TFC parents daily information about the child's attendance, his behavior in class, homework completion, and any missing assignments or tests. The card is designed to make it easy for teachers to complete quickly. In some instances, the school contact person may request some modifications in the card to fit the particular setting. An example is shown in Table 7.1.

After reviewing the school card, the contact person is asked to distribute it to all of the adolescent's teachers. The teachers are encouraged to call the case manager if they have any questions or concerns about using the school card. Once school begins, it is the child's responsibility to have the teachers fill out the card every day. The card is then brought home, and points are added or subtracted depending on the information provided by the teachers. The

**Table 7.1
School Card**

Student's Name _____ Date _____

Class	Today's Assignment	Assignment Turned In	Overdue Homework*	Tardy	Behavior	Teacher's Initials
1		Y / N	Y / N	Y / N	Good / Poor	
2		Y / N	Y / N	Y / N	Good / Poor	
3		Y / N	Y / N	Y / N	Good / Poor	
4		Y / N	Y / N	Y / N	Good / Poor	
5		Y / N	Y / N	Y / N	Good / Poor	
6		Y / N	Y / N	Y / N	Good / Poor	
7		Y / N	Y / N	Y / N	Good / Poor	

*Please identify overdue homework on the back of this form.

child is thoroughly briefed on the procedure for giving the school card to his teachers. We arrange to have the TFC parent assist in this task by role-playing with the teenager the process of presenting the card to the teacher. The TFC parent also makes contacts with the teachers and actually goes to school with the adolescent, if necessary. We find that the school card is an excellent way to exchange information between teachers and TFC parents.

As one might expect, problems do arise with using the school card. These include the youth's forging signatures and falsifying information, teachers becoming annoyed with having to complete the card every day, teachers feeling that nothing productive is being done with the information they provide, and the child feeling embarrassed at having to get the card signed. Of course, the best way to deal with these problems is to anticipate them and do the groundwork necessary to prevent them.

School cards should be regularly monitored for falsified information. Weekly contact with the school counselor or one or more teachers is usually sufficient to verify the information supplied for the previous week. The TFC parents are open with the child in stating that "the program has me check on your school card." This keeps the process aboveboard and seems to help the adolescent resist the temptation to forge signatures. Typically, the youth loses points for not getting all the required signatures. The case manager also checks with the school to be sure the child did not miss all or part of a class. If the child continues to fail to get teachers to sign the school card, the foster parent or case manager accompanies him to school. The consequences for falsifying information on the school card usually include work chores, demotion to a lower level in the point system, and restriction of privileges.

At first, it may be difficult to get teachers to cooperate with filling out the card. In this situation, the case manager should contact the teacher by telephone and explain why the information is being collected and how it is used. A teacher who dislikes the card may be more likely to use it if he or she is encouraged to modify the card format. After two or three weeks of filling out the school card, teachers might begin to doubt whether it is helpful; this is often due to their unrealistic expectations. Our initial expectations are modest, given that most of the youngsters we work with have severe and long-standing school problems. If the child attends classes regularly, is not tardy, is reasonably well behaved in class, and completes most of the homework, we are satisfied. When the adolescent is successful with this level of performance, we begin to emphasize academic achievement. The expectations of teachers may be somewhat higher. Often the teenager's current performance can be put into perspective by discussing the student's history with the teacher. Specific information about the child's past problems is shared with teachers to the extent the case manager feels it will help them deal with him.

At first, it may be embarrassing for the child to ask his teachers to fill out the school card. The TFC parents do their best to reassure the child and provide emotional support. They also acknowledge that it must be difficult to do this every day but point out that the adolescent earns points for his efforts. Although the foster parents are empathetic, they should not waver on the issue of whether the school card is necessary. The use of the card is a program rule. TFC parents can tell the child that if he does well in school for a certain period of time, they will ask the case manager to change to a once-per-week school card system. Typically, the child's embarrassment subsides once he actually uses the card for a day or two.

PAROLE OR PROBATION STAFF LIAISON

With court-mandated cases, it is essential to coordinate the adolescent's treatment plan with the persons who are making decisions about the consequences for illegal behavior and parole or probation violations. The first step is to establish a set of operating assumptions that both the program staff and parole workers can agree upon. These assumptions usually include the following: (1) the types and severity of consequences to be imposed by the program for major rule breaking or legal infractions, (2) how detention will be used, (3) the roles program and parole staff will take relative to one another in their interactions with the teenager and his family, and (4) the frequency and setting in which contacts will take place with the youth, his biological or adoptive parents, and the parole worker. In our TFC programs, these ground rules were initially discussed in a series of meetings with the case managers, the program director, and the county parole officers. Since that time, the rules have been modified to accommodate the needs of the adolescents and families we work with.

Many of these issues are difficult to address when a TFC program is just getting started. At that point, the effectiveness of the program has not been demonstrated, and parole workers are often skeptical about the ability of the TFC approach to deal with delinquents. With a little flexibility and creativity, however, new ways to work together develop as the program progresses. Our first attempts to build good working agreements with parole staff brought mixed results. The breakthrough came when we put case managers (rather than therapists) fully in charge of developing and maintaining relations with parole workers.

As we have mentioned earlier, consequences are prespecified for common types of rule violations, such as being late or unsupervised, drug and alcohol use, minor law infractions, and suspension or expulsion from school. These consequences are preset to handle a typical violation, but they can be changed to fit a special situation. Establishing preset consequences helps the parole worker feel comfortable with the idea of allowing the program to routinely deal with infractions. In serious or chronic cases of rule breaking, the active support of the parole worker can make a critical difference. The role of the parole worker can come into play during an intervention for rule breaking in several different ways. The following case example provides an example of a dramatic intervention.

CASE EXAMPLE: JIMMY DECIDES TO SKIP SCHOOL

Jimmy liked to avoid confrontations. Instead of being compliant, his approach was to be overtly agreeable and then do as he pleased. At the age of 15, Jimmy had little interest in school. During the past week, he had skipped several classes on two separate days. The first episode occurred on Monday, and Jimmy was given a work chore that consisted of two hours of work for each class missed. Because he missed three classes, the consequence was six hours of work. He also was put on Level 1 until the work chore was completed. Jimmy managed to finish the work chore in two days without much stalling or delay; the TFC parents and program staff were pleased with his cooperation. Then on Thursday he skipped again. This time, he was seen with another boy downtown. This was clearly a high-risk situation for Jimmy because he had an extensive history of burglary and shoplifting.

The case manager and the parole worker had a telephone conference to discuss the options.

Jimmy could be given another work chore, but that did not seem strong enough by itself to get his attention. They could put him in detention, but the detention center was full and it was hard to justify the use of detention for a noncrime violation such as skipping classes. They also had to decide whether Jimmy would be allowed to go for his home visit scheduled on Friday. The family therapist wanted Jimmy to have the visit because she was concerned that his parents were beginning to drift away from him. In their last therapy session, she had taught his parents how to use the point chart and arranged to have them participate in a fun activity with Jimmy.

The case manager and the parole worker decided to implement a three-step plan. The case manager called the TFC parents and told them about the plan and immediately had them bring Jimmy in for a meeting. At the meeting, the case manager told Jimmy that he had an eight-hour work chore and that he was on Level 1 until it was completed. Also, he would not be able to go on his home visit unless the chore was completed by Friday at 8:00 p.m. Just then, the parole worker came in and handcuffed Jimmy and said that he was taking him to detention. The case manager said, "Look, I think we should give Jimmy another chance. He admitted that he skipped classes and has agreed to do an eight-hour work chore. Right, Jimmy?"

Jimmy quickly agreed.

The parole officer said, "Tell me why a work chore will teach him anything? He just finished doing one earlier this week, didn't he?"

The case manager responded with, "That's a good point — I don't know what to say about that. What about you, Jimmy?"

Although his approach was somewhat unpolished, Jimmy came to his own defense, "I'll do it. I won't cut anymore — you guys always catch me."

The parole worker agreed to try the work chore "one more time" but made it clear he had his doubts about whether it would work. Then he left. Once they were alone, the case manager told Jimmy she was relieved the situation turned out as well as it did and made a point of mentioning that it was a "close call." She told Jimmy that he should talk to his therapist that evening to discuss how he could avoid cutting classes in the future, confirmed that she would have the therapist call, and sent him home to start the work chore. Jimmy finished his work chore in time to go on his home visit as scheduled. The intervention seemed to make a lasting impression on Jimmy. He stayed in school from that point on and eventually graduated from the program.

LIAISON WITH JUDGES

In our county, the position of juvenile judge is usually rotated every year. This creates problems, because just when you get to know one judge, someone else steps in. During the last few years we have developed the following procedure to familiarize each new judge with our program. At the beginning of judge's term, we send a written description of the program and a letter of introduction asking for an appointment. Then we make a follow-up phone call and explain that we would like to meet with the judge for 30 minutes when it is convenient. The program director and one or two case managers attend the meeting. We prepare a brief description of the program and send it to the judge in advance. The description states who we serve, the overall structure and philosophy of the program, and who to contact for referrals or further information. At the meeting, the judge is invited to ask questions and discuss the treatment model. Then we clarify other issues that are likely to come up, such as when the judge would like us to appear in court (e.g., when the youth is originally mandated to the program and at any subsequent hearings). We tell the judge to feel free to contact us if the way we are implementing the program or our recommendations to the court cause any problems. This usually sets the stage for cooperation. At the end of the judge's term, we ask the departing judge to introduce and recommend our program to the incoming judge.

SUMMARY

An important part of the case manager's job is to identify and work with key individuals in the community who have contact with or influence on the child. In all cases, this includes school personnel: teachers, guidance counselors, assistant principals, school psychologists, and other school staff who interact with the child. The first order of business in the school is to set up a system to monitor the child's behavior and academic progress to prevent problems from occurring and to deal with problems before they become serious. This system minimizes suspensions or expulsions, which can be a serious problem in working with a group of youngsters who tend to act out in school or avoid school entirely.

Collaborating with the child's parole or probation officer is another key component of case management. Fostering a good working relationship prevents conflicts about case disposition, and it sends a stronger, more consistent message to the child. Finally, if an outside authority such as a judge or referee is making decisions about case disposition, it is essential for the case manager to establish a collaborative relationship with that person as well. Other community agencies or individuals that may require attention from the case manager are employers, coaches, or other treatment agents. The idea is to pull together all the threads of influence and contact the child experiences day to day in the community and weave these into the child's treatment plan.

8

AFTERCARE SERVICES FOR CHILDREN AND FAMILIES

The transition back home is a risky time for adolescents who have participated in residential care programs. In the Monitor Program, approximately 85% of the teenagers return home; of these, 75% live with their parents and 10% live with relatives. Immediately following the return home, both the parents and the child often experience a "honeymoon period" during which things go reasonably well. This can be a dangerous time in that the parents tend to overlook small rule infractions and problem behaviors and to let the teenager's good behavior go unnoticed as well. Gradually, the adolescent realizes that the situation at home is much the same as it was before the placement. The lack of close supervision means that consequences are not used consistently, and it usually takes only a short time for the adolescent to drift into associating with delinquent peers and participating in delinquent activities again. When the parents become aware of this, often painfully following another arrest, they can quickly slip back into thinking that "nothing has changed" and be at-risk for giving up. To counteract this all too familiar scenario, we have developed an aftercare component to the Monitor Program that begins when the child returns home and continues for twelve months. This chapter reviews the rationale for and treatment services offered in aftercare.

REDUCING THE RISKS ASSOCIATED WITH TRANSITIONS

Transitions are notoriously difficult and risky times for children. This finding has been well documented in programmatic prevention studies (e.g., Coddington 1972; Felner, Farber, & Primavera 1983; Felner, Primavera, & Couce 1981). Even minor transitions such as moving a child from one classroom to another can create new problems; for example, the new setting may be less structured, or the child may test the limits in the new class. Certainly, a change in parenting figures is a major transition; it is not surprising that this transition has been shown to be associated with depression and conduct problems in adolescents (Capaldi 1991; Capaldi & Patterson 1991).

For TFC children, the transition from the foster home back to their natural or adoptive family carries with it a myriad of risks. It often involves returning to a school setting where they associated with antisocial peers and their academic performance was marginal at best (Moore & Chamberlain 1994). Although these children have experienced a change in the way their natural or adoptive parents set limits and supervise them during home visits, they often test their parents to find out whether these changes are permanent when they return home. As one 14-year-old boy said about his imminent return home, "Finally, I get to go back to normal life, where I can do whatever I want and not have anyone tell me I have to be here or there, or do this or that." Before he was referred to the TFC program, he slept during the day, stayed out all night, and rarely attended school. It was a formidable task for the program to help him adjust to leading a more mainstream "normal life."

Ironically, state funding stops when the child makes the transition back home, yet this is the time when both child and parents need the most support. This dilemma prompted us to write a grant to conduct a research and demonstration project that would focus on reunification of children and parents.

Early in our aftercare work with parents and children we discovered that the families who seemed to need these services the most were the least likely to actually use them. It soon became clear these people faced barriers that made it difficult for them to make plans and keep appointments. We decided that the only way we could have an affect on these reunified families would be to accept a new level of responsibility for delivering services to them; instead of assuming that their lack of follow-through was *their* problem, we made it *our* problem. Delivering aftercare services means actually getting those services to the client. If you wait for them to come to you, nothing happens.

TEACHING AND SUPPORTING FAMILIES IN AFTERCARE

In 1990 a three-component model for family reunification was funded by the Children's Bureau at the federal Department of Health and Human Services (Teaching and Supporting Families: A Model for Reunification; Award #90CW0994, DHHS, 1990 – 1993). This grant has allowed us to refine our approach to delivering relevant and effective aftercare services. The project was funded for three years, ending in 1993. The components included (1) support for parenting and parent training, including group and individual contacts; (2) "coaching" of the child in key social and relationship skills; and (3) respite days, allowing the parents to take a break by caring for their children in one of our TFC homes.

We provide ongoing support and education for parents in several ways. One of the primary vehicles is weekly group meetings. The meetings facilitate three primary goals: (1) to provide information and refine parenting skills that were emphasized during the TFC family therapy sessions, (2) to give the parents support for their child management efforts, and (3) to identify barriers to effective parenting. Individual family therapy sessions are offered to parents who are having extreme difficulties or facing crises or who request additional help. In addition, parents are contacted daily (M – F) by telephone to collect data on their teenager's adjustment during the past 24 hours, using the Parent Daily Report checklist described in Chapter 10. Extra time is allowed during this brief contact to debrief any problems, acknowledge successes, and troubleshoot anticipated problems. Generally, the call is made by therapists or case managers, but we have also found that foster parent trainers with experience as program foster parents also do a good job.

Parent Group Meetings

As previously mentioned, it was difficult at first to get parents to attend group meetings. Even when we provided child care services and money for transportation, many parents dreaded the thought of participating in a group and avoided the meetings. Our next step was to make the group more appealing. In their prevention research with high-risk inner city mothers, Byron Egeland and his colleagues found that serving a meal during group time encouraged participation (Pianta 1990). When we tried this with our groups, more parents started coming to the meetings. We also instituted a drawing for $15 at the end of each meeting. Later, we extended this to two drawings; parents who simply attended the group meeting were eligible for the first $10 drawing, and those who completed their home practice assignment that week were eligible for a second $10 drawing. These changes substantially improved group attendance. Interestingly enough, group leaders felt it was not just receiving the money and the meal that promoted attendance; the meal and a chance to win the drawing gave parents a face-saving excuse for attending the sessions.

Groups usually consist of five to seven parents or sets of parents. Group sessions last one hour, and parents usually attend the meetings for the first 12 months of the aftercare period. The meetings are conducted by two group leaders who have extensive experience with the TFC model; one of the leaders can be a junior therapist. Having two leaders allows for more flexibility in presenting and reviewing the material with the parents. For example, we find that role-playing is often a more effective way to teach skills than discussions or lectures. However, parents are often shy at first, and asking them to role-play too soon can scare them away. The two leaders can do the role-playing themselves, and if they work well together the exercises are entertaining and provide effective modeling for parents.

The core curriculum consists of 25 sessions; 5 on encouragement and confidence building for both parent and child, 5 on teaching new behaviors, 5 on setting limits, 3 on promoting school success, 2 on problem solving, and 5 on stress management and utilizing community support and services. Although there is a set "lesson plan" for each session (Chamberlain & Antoine, in preparation), unstructured time is allowed for group interaction, discussing problems, and offering support. It is best if parents can go through each of these sessions twice, and the year-long time frame allows for this. The first time they participate in the sessions, they are adjusting to having their child back at home. The second time through (about six months later) parents are usually facing related but different issues, and they are in a good position to offer advice to new parents in the group.

Leaders must be sensitive to group process issues. The goal is to strike a balance among giving support, allowing for individualization, and providing instruction. This promotes a feeling of comfort and safety for group members. Group leaders are available by telephone between sessions if the parents want to discuss an urgent issue.

"Coaching" Sessions

The individual therapy sessions for the adolescent were described in Chapter 5. The emphasis of the sessions shifts in aftercare. The individual sessions in aftercare combine recreational or "fun" activities out in the community with helping the child deal with problems that he encounters at home, in school, or in the community. To make the sessions feel less clinical and give the child a sense of progress, the staff members who conduct these sessions are called "community coaches." Coaches are individuals who have experience dealing with adolescents and training in mental health, psychology, or related fields.

The format for the sessions involves filling out a weekly "scorecard" and participating in activities together. The scorecards are developed jointly by the coach and the child and list four or five behaviors that the child has reported are difficult for him. An example is shown in Table 8.1. Once every week, the teenager rates how well he did on each behavior during the past week using a 10-point scale. The coach and adolescent select a behavior (usually the one with the lowest score) to work on during the next week. Then they develop a "game plan" that includes identifying specific behaviors or activities for the child to practice. The coach tries to set up opportunities to rehearse or role-play one or more of these behaviors during the activity portion of the coaching session.

The purpose of this contact is to help the adolescents identify problem areas and to plan and practice strategies for dealing with them. Also, they are asked to reflect on their behavior during the past week and recognize their successes as well as areas in which they need improvement. The relationship between the coach and child should be a supportive one that builds on the child's areas of interest, encourages him to participate in prosocial activities in the community, and develops interpersonal and recreational skills. The coach assists the child in choosing "fun" activities. Teenagers with a history of severe problems often have a striking lack of interest and experience in normal activities such as sports, hobbies, and games. The coach serves as a resource and stimulus to help the child sample new activities. In some instances, we try to match coaches with children based on common interests, for example, fishing or roller skating. Coaches are most often, but not always, the same gender as the children they work with.

This component of the aftercare program is based, in large part, on a project conducted in Holland from 1984 to 1987 (Beljaars & Berger 1988). Investigators found that compared with a group that was not coached, the 32 adolescents who had received weekly coaching were rated as most improved in the areas of problems and peer relations. The research design did have some flaws; the ratings were made by caseworkers who could have been influenced by their knowledge of which youths had participated in the coaching project, and the comparison group was not randomly assigned. Nonetheless, this seemed to us to be a promising approach. It is our impression that coaching has been successful in our program as well. Although we have not studied the contribution of the coaching component and do not have scientific evidence on its effectiveness, the teenagers report that they enjoy the sessions, and their parents consistently say they are pleased with their child's participation in the coaching sessions.

Table 8.1
Jeff's Weekly Scorecard

Week of _____

Behavior	Score*
Turning in daily math homework	
Not arguing with mom	
Avoiding Chet at lunch break	
Reading and relaxing	

*Give yourself a score from 1 to 10. How did you do on each of these during the past week? If you did great, give yourself a 10. If you did poorly, give yourself a 1. Or, give yourself a score between 1 and 10.

CASE EXAMPLE: LEE LEARNS AN IMPORTANT LESSON

For most of his life, Lee had experienced problems with hyperactivity and peer relations. He had been diagnosed as having Attention Deficit Hyperactivity Disorder at age 5 and had been on and off medications for this disorder for 10 years. Now at age 15, he had completed the Monitor Program and was returning home to live with his mother and twin brother. He had been referred to the program because of a series of neighborhood thefts he committed and high levels of conflict at home, including his violent attacks on his mother and brother. During his stay at the foster home, he had substantially improved his ability to regulate his temper by developing alternative strategies, such as taking a short "time out" when he felt himself becoming angry. He still had problems with talking over others and interrupting. This, as might be expected, caused him to alienate peers, and he became the target of teasing and rejection.

Lee had listed five areas for improvement on his scorecard: getting along with Mom, getting along with Larry (his twin), making friends, not interrupting teachers, and earning money. He rated himself lowest (a score of 2) in the area of friends. When Lee's coach talked to him about how he could work on improving this, it was clear that Lee did not know where to begin. The coach suggested two things he thought were important for making friends: listening without interrupting and then making a statement of agreement or understanding, and deflecting teasing or put-downs by laughing.

In a situation such as this, the coach should limit and carefully define which skills the child works on. Lee wanted to practice both skills at the same time. This would have been overwhelming for him, and he would have ended up learning neither skill. Lee decided to begin by practicing the second skill for a week. Then Lee and his coach went to a basketball court to shoot hoops. On the way there, the coach told Lee to tease him (the coach) and put him down so that he could show Lee how to shrug it off. The purpose was to model this behavior for Lee. After doing this a few times, the coach said, "Okay, let's switch. Now I'll give you a hard time, and let's see how it goes." When the roles were reversed, Lee copied the coach's responses almost exactly. In many cases, this demonstration-based approach to teaching skills is more effective than talking with adolescents about making changes.

RESPITE CARE

Originally, we planned to offer weekend respite care for program youths whose parents had attended 75% of the parent group sessions. We thought parents would be eager to earn respite services, and it could be used as an incentive for participating in the parent groups. As it turned out, this was a poor incentive because parents did not want to use weekend respite unless they were having severe problems, which meant they were more likely to miss parent group meetings. We soon decided to change our approach.

Now parents are told that periodic respite weekends are available to them during times of stress or if they simply need a break. We employ one foster family on a part-time basis for this purpose; sometimes they are new treatment foster parents who are waiting for a placement, or occasionally the original treatment foster parents who provided the program placement for the child are available for weekend respite.

We are often asked whether parents tend to overuse and abuse the privilege of respite care. Our experience has been quite the opposite. Parents and children avoid using respite weekends unless they need it. If things are going well with their child, respite is a disruption from the parent's point of view. If there is a problem, the parents are often reluctant to give the child a "vacation" or escape in respite. Although we have not evaluated the importance of offering respite care, it is our clinical impression that it is a useful resource.

CUSTOMIZING AFTERCARE SERVICES

At first, we tried to fit families into the interventions that we offered in aftercare. Then we realized that we would have better participation if we fitted the services to the needs of the families. Matching services to case needs is the underpinning of the wrap-around model of service delivery advocated by Karl W. Dennis (1992) and others. The concept is that treatment plans should be case-driven rather than determined by the services available. The reality is that funding regulations often limit how programs can use their resources. However, the Office of Special Education Programs Division of Innovation and Development is interested in the development of "family friendly" service models. A recent grant from this agency has allowed us to experiment with fitting services to family needs (Family Alliances Change Teens, 1992 – 1994; Award #H237E20018). A few examples of our attempts to customize services are having a telephone installed in the home to help the parents and program staff monitor the child's behavior at school and in the community, conducting in-home therapy sessions, paying for special needs and fees, providing academic tutoring, having an observer/interventionist in the schools, giving parents and children rewards such as a "movie night out" for special accomplishments, paying for music lessons, and providing funds for transportation and child care.

SUMMARY

It is our impression that the child's chances of success are enhanced by offering aftercare services to both the child and his parents. Following the teenager's return home, we continue our contact with the parent through weekly group meetings, regular telephone contact (including data collection), and other services such as family therapy sessions as needed. For the child, there is a definite shift in the nature of the aftercare contact. Instead of therapy sessions, the youth is assigned a community "coach" who teaches him social and relational skills in a learning-by-doing format. This coaching makes the transition back home less disruptive and helps reprogram the child's social environment. A research project now under way is designed to give us additional insights into how these services should be delivered and which components are effective.

9

OUTCOME EVALUATION OF TREATMENT FOSTER CARE PROGRAM PARTICIPANTS

The relative effectiveness of our TFC model has been evaluated in two studies. These studies compared the case outcomes for children and teenagers who participated in our programs with outcomes of those who were in other community-based placements. In the first study (Chamberlain 1990), 16 TFC cases were matched with youths placed in other community-based programs who were also referred because of chronic delinquency. In the second study (Chamberlain & Reid 1991), a more powerful, random assignment design was used to compare the success of TFC treatment with placement in other community-based settings for psychiatrically disturbed youngsters who were leaving the state mental hospital.

STUDY 1: EFFECTIVENESS OF TFC FOR DELINQUENT YOUTH

TFC cases referred for delinquency were matched by age, sex, and date of commitment to the state training school[1] with a group of youths who were court-referred to other treatment settings. The matching was conducted with the assistance of the research department at the state Children's Services Division.[2] A complete description of the procedures used in the study and the results are provided in Chamberlain (1990); an overview and summary are presented here.

---

[1]. When the TFC program was first funded, all of the youths had to have been committed to one of the two state training schools to be admitted. For the past seven years, however, that requirement has been dropped and precommitment youths who are at-risk for training school placement can be admitted as well.

[2]. Cecil Hinsley and Don Grossnickle from CSD collaborated on this project.

The participants were 6 girls and 10 boys who had been referred to the Monitor Program by the courts. All had been officially committed to one of Oregon's two state training schools and then diverted to the Monitor Program. The matched comparison subjects were drawn from a pool of 435 youths who had been committed and diverted to community programs throughout the state. A computer program was written to do the matching using demographic information coded from the case files. Table 9.1 shows data on family risk factors, child risk factors, child dangerousness, and school adjustment for each group. As shown in Table 9.1, the subjects were comparable on 18 of the 19 characteristics examined. A difference was found in the proportion of cases that had been adopted ($p < .02$; TFC greater than comparison). Overall, however, the characteristics of the two groups were comparable.

Of the 16 matched subjects, 8 were placed

Table 9.1
Subject Characteristics

Demographic and Risk Factors	Experimental		Control	
Average age	14.56		14.56	
Sex	10M, 6F		10M, 6F	
Average # of prior out-of-home placements	1.75 (range 0 – 8)		1.31 (range 0 – 5)	
Family risk factors				
Family income below poverty level	8/16	(50%)	10/16	(63%)
Divorce of natural parents*	16/16	(100%)	12/16	(75%)
Three or more siblings	6/16	(38%)	10/16	(67%)
Adopted*	5/16	(31%)	0/16	(0%)
Parent hospitalized (current or previous)	1/16	(6%)	1/16	(6%)
Parent convicted of felony (current or previous)	2/16	(13%)	1/16	(6%)
Siblings institutionalized (current or previous)	2/16	(13%)	2/16	(13%)
Family available for aftercare	10/16	(63%)	11/16	(69%)
Child risk factors				
Physically abused (reported)	6/16	(38%)	7/16	(44%)
Sexually abused (reported)	2/16	(13%)	2/16	(13%)
Chronic runaway (less than 3 priors)	7/16	(44%)	8/16	(50%)
Suicide attempts	4/16	(25%)	3/16	(19%)
Child dangerousness				
Sexually abusive — adjudicated	3/16	(19%)	3/16	(19%)
Previous felony charge	11/16	(69%)	10/16	(63%)
Dangerous to others	4/16	(25%)	5/16	(31%)
Dangerous to self	6/16	(38%)	4/16	(25%)
Child school adjustment				
Chronic truancy	12/16	(75%)	12/16	(75%)
Below grade level (at year 1)	9/16	(56%)	10/16	(63%)

*$p < .02$

in group homes, 4 in a secure residential center specializing in drug and alcohol treatment, 2 in their parents' homes with intensive parole supervision, and 2 in another program based on the TFC model in Monmouth, Oregon.[3]

Case outcomes were tracked in several ways, including data on program completion and subsequent incarceration using CSD service records. The service records have good validity in that they are used as the basis for payment

---

[3]. This is the Mentor Program, directed by Mavis Chitwood.

for all child and adolescent placements made by CSD. Their accuracy is therefore rigorously monitored on an ongoing basis for program providers and caseworkers. CSD service records were reviewed to obtain the following information for three time periods: (1) the number of days the youth had been incarcerated during the 12 months prior to placement in a community program, (2) the number of days the youth had participated in the community program during treatment, and (3) the number of days the youth was incarcerated during the two years posttreatment. These data were coded independently by two research assistants for each of the three time periods; the intercoder agreement was 96%.

During pretreatment, of the 16 cases in the Monitor Program, 12 had been previously incarcerated in the state training school, as had 12 of the comparison cases. The average number of days incarcerated during preplacement was 29.2 for Monitor Program cases and 14.9 for comparison cases. The difference was not statistically significant.

During treatment, no difference was found in the average amount of therapy received by the subjects in the two groups. Monitor Program cases were in treatment for an average of 142 days (S.D. = 78; range, 15 – 264 days) and the average for comparison cases was 146 days (S.D. = 112; range, 15 – 414 days). The data on treatment completion status are shown in Table 9.2. Twelve (75%) of the 16 Monitor Program cases completed their six-month programs, 3 (19%) had their parole revoked and were incarcerated, and 1 (6%) ran away. For the comparison cases, 5 (31%) completed their programs, 4 (25%) were revoked, and 7 (44%) ran away. The rate of successful versus unsuccessful program completion was different for the two groups, favoring cases in the Monitor Program (chi-square = 6.15; p < .03). It is interesting to note that both of the cases placed in the Mon-

Table 9.2
Treatment Completion

Completion Status	Experimental	Control
Completed Program	12 (75%)	5 (31%)
Failed to complete		
Incarcerated	3 (19%)	4 (25%)
Ran away	1 (6%)	7 (44%)

mouth TFC program successfully completed the program; that number represented 40% of the successful control completers.

Follow-up data on the number of days incarcerated posttreatment showed a difference between the groups. During the first year posttreatment, 6 of the 16 Monitor Program cases (38%) and 14 of the 16 control cases (88%) were incarcerated (chi-square = 6.53; $p = .01$). Although a smaller proportion of the cases in both groups were institutionalized during the year after (versus the year before) treatment, the average number of days increased for those who were incarcerated (Monitor Program: pre = 22.9, post = 86.4; control: pre = 14.9, post = 159.9). At the rate of $75 per day, the first-year cost to the state for the 6 incarcerated Monitor Program cases was $103,650, and the comparable figure for the 14 control cases was $191,850; the difference in cost between the two groups was more than $88,000.

The findings were similar for the second year of follow-up. Seven of the original 16 Monitor Program cases were incarcerated, as were 10 of 16 control cases. The difference in costs for incarceration was $122,000, favoring the Monitor Program cases. The cumulative number of days incarcerated and associated costs are shown in Figure 9.1. During the first year of follow-up, Monitor Program cases spent an average of 46% fewer days incarcerated than controls; in the second year, the average was 34% fewer days. When the data for

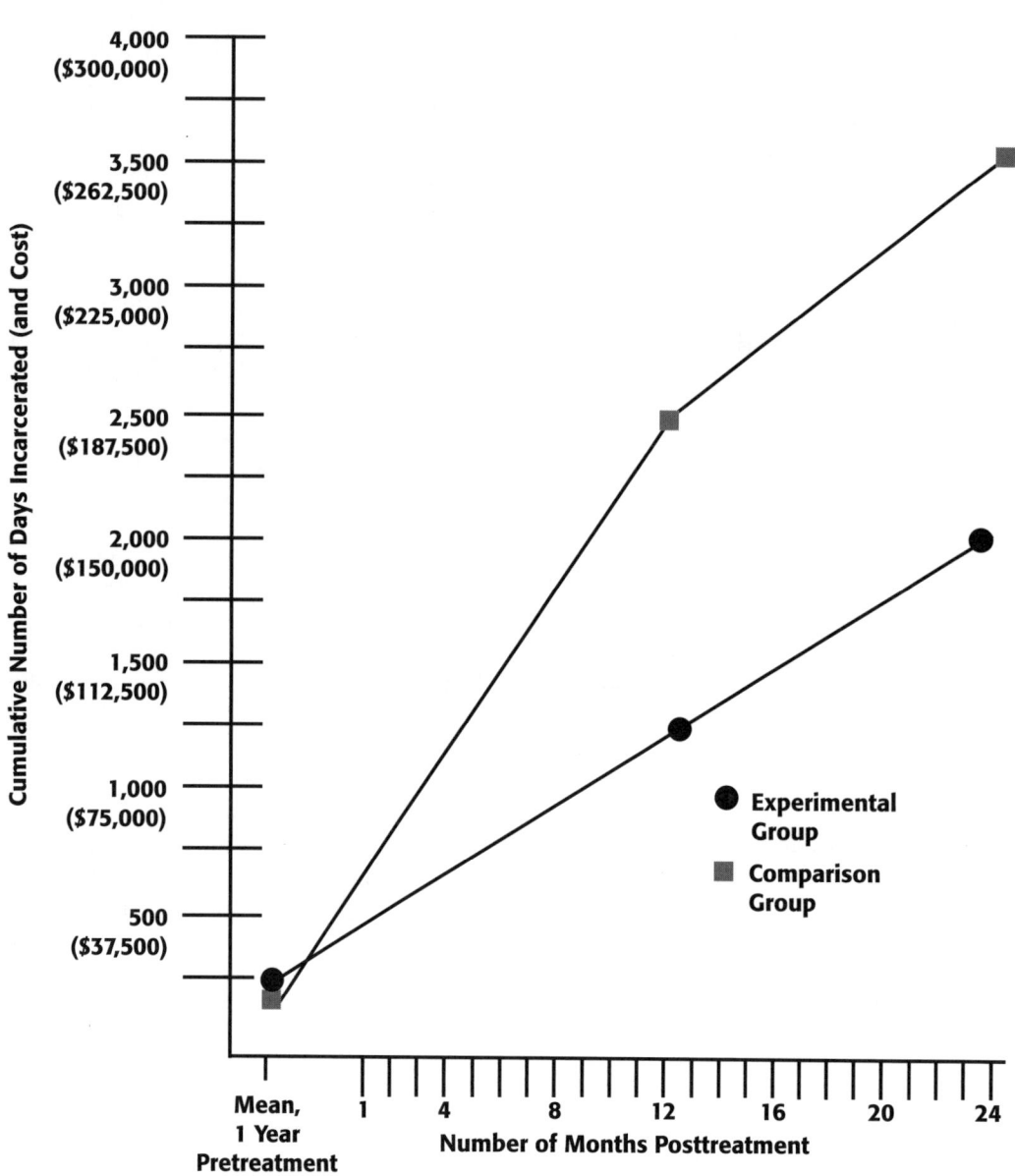

**Figure 9.1
Incarceration Data**

both years were combined, we found that 50% of the Monitor Program youths had been incarcerated at some time; the comparable figure for controls was 94%. This difference was statistically significant (chi-square = 5.56; $p = .018$).

We also examined the relation between the length of treatment and subsequent incarceration. These data are shown in Figure 9.2. Did longer periods of treatment relate to less time in jail during follow-up? A significant correlation was found for the Monitor Program group ($r = -.72$; $p = .001$) but not for the control group ($r = .04$, N.S.). In addition, the more days Monitor Program cases spent in the program, the fewer days they spent in jail during the two years of follow-up that we studied. This "dosage effect" is indirect evidence for the effectiveness of the Monitor Program treatment.

Although the findings from this study are promising, it is difficult to draw conclusions because the design is weak. We cannot rule out the possibility that control cases, although matched on three important variables, might have been substantively different from Monitor Program cases on other variables. The next study used a stronger experimental design and focused on a more seriously disturbed population of children and adolescents.

STUDY 2: TFC FOR EMOTIONALLY DISTURBED YOUTHS

In late 1985, the director of the Oregon State Hospital Child and Adolescent Treatment Program (CATP) asked if we would be interested in applying our TFC model to the patients in his programs. The problem in this setting was that despite vigorous community outreach efforts, it was difficult to find community-based programs that were equipped to deal with the unique individual needs of the children and adolescents that they were discharging. Many of the youngsters did not have family or relatives available as resources at discharge, or their families were judged to be too disturbed or disorganized to be able to provide for the complex needs of their children.

If residential centers took these youngsters at all, they typically designated only one or two slots for CATP graduates. This decision was largely due to the risk involved and the potential

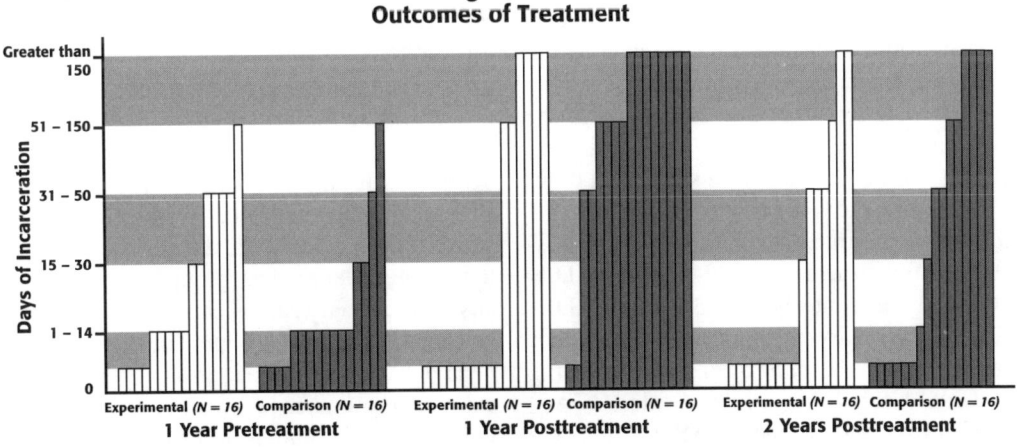

**Figure 9.2
Outcomes of Treatment**

*Each column represents 1 subject in sample.

for disruptive influence on the other program residents. We thought that the individualized planning and flexibility offered by the TFC model could make this service delivery system an effective alternative if foster parents could be trained and supervised to deal with severely psychiatrically disturbed children and teens.

To examine this possibility, we applied for funding to conduct a controlled study that compared TFC to the existing treatments available in the community. Our proposal was funded in 1986 by the Children's Bureau (DHHS Grant #90CW0803), and the program was subsequently operated for 2.5 years. Participants were referred to the study by outreach teams at CATP. The multidisciplinary teams included staff who had worked with each case (e.g., psychiatrists, psychologists, social workers, group workers, occupational therapists, educators). All of the referred cases were judged to be ready for discharge to a community placement. After referral, study participants were randomly assigned to the experimental (i.e., Treatment Foster Care) or control (i.e., treatment as usual) conditions.

Descriptive data were collected on the 20 participants, who were 9 to 18 years of age. One 18-year-old female refused to participate. Table 9.3 shows demographic data, risk factors, and special clinical issues for the subjects in each group. Table 9.4 provides data on the sex, age, IQ, and diagnosis of the subjects.

These data highlight the seriousness of the problems experienced by the study children. All but 6 of the 20 participants had dual diagnoses. During the year prior to admission to the study, the experimental subjects had been hospitalized for an average of 245 days (S.D. = 105), and the controls for 236 days (S.D. = 125). The severity of emotional disturbance was evaluated at baseline by expert raters using the Child Global Assessment Scale (CGAS) (Shaffer et al. 1983). The CGAS measures the level of functioning for an individual during the past month; the scale has been shown to have good psychometric properties, including stability and concurrent and discriminate validity. Raters were senior psychiatric residents who were blind to group assignment. On the average, study cases fell into the category of "major impairment in functioning in several areas." This category indicates that the cases were judged to have exhibited severely disturbed behavior across several settings (e.g., home, school, and community).

At baseline, and then at three and six months later, the following measures were administered to study participants:

1. Institutionalization rates. Three time periods were assessed for all subjects: (a) the year prior to referral to the study, (b) the time from referral to placement outside the hospital, and (c) the period beginning with placement through the next 365 days. The rate of days institutionalized was considered to be the primary or "bottom line" indicator of success or failure for these cases.

2. The Behavior Symptom Inventory (BSI; Derogatis & Spencer 1982). The BSI is a self-report inventory that asks children to rate their level of symptoms and distress. The Global Severity Index score, which has been shown to have good test-retest stability, was used.

3. The Parent Daily Report checklist (PDR; Chamberlain & Reid 1987). This checklist measures the occurrence of problems and symptoms during the prior 24-hour time period. PDR data were collected by telephone from ward staff on 10 separate days at baseline, and then from foster parents, group home staff, and any other primary caretaker of the child at three and six months postbaseline. The PDR problem behavior score has been used in numerous clinical outcome studies (e.g., Patterson 1974; Patterson, Chamberlain, & Reid 1982) and it has been adapted for use with families in Italy

Table 9.3
Demographic Data

	Treatment Group		Control Group	
Youth admitted	10 (5M, 5 F)		10 (3M, 7 F)	
Average age	13.9 (range 9 – 18)		15.1 (range 12 – 17)	
Average number of out-of-home placements	5.1 (range 1 – 10)		5.0 (range 1 – 12)	
Family makeup				
Divorced	7/9	(77%)	8/9	(88%)
Failed adoptions	3/10	(30%)		
Siblings institutionalized	2/10	(20%)	3/10	(30%)
Siblings in foster care	5/10	(50%)	4/10	(40%)
History of family mental illness or in institutions	8/10	(80%)	9/10	(90%)
Family as aftercare resource	0/10	(0%)	2/10	(20%)
Risk variables				
Family at poverty level	5/10	(50%)	6/10	(60%)
Family violence	8/10	(80%)	9/10	(90%)
Three or more siblings	5/10	(50%)	4/10	(40%)
Youth with record of felonies (documented)	3/10	(30%)	3/10	(30%)
Youth with physical attacks on others (documented)	6/10	(60%)	5/10	(50%)
Sexually abusive	4/10	(40%)	2/10	(20%)
Fire setting	1/10	(10%)	1/10	(10%)
History of law violations (adjudicated)	5/10	(50%)	4/10	(40%)
Special clinical concerns				
Suicide attempts	6/10	(60%)	2/10	(20%)
Drug/alcohol dependency	3/10	(30%)	5/10	(50%)
Multiple runaways	6/10	(60%)	8/10	(80%)
Chronic truancy	4/10	(40%)	7/10	(70%)
Sexually abused	8/10	(80%)	7/10	(70%)

Source: Chamberlain and Reid 1991, p. 286.
Copyright 1991. Printed by permission from Clinical Psychology Publishing Co., Brandon, VT.

(Pastorelli 1992) and Canada (Hunt, Day, & Levene 1991). PDR has good reliability and validity, and normative data are available on a nonreferred population of 4- to 12-year-old children.

4. The Social Interaction Task. This is a structured task designed to assess social skill and problem-solving ability. Several different instruments were used, depending on the child's age. For youths 12 years of age and

Table 9.4
Sex, Age, IQ, and Diagnosis of Subjects

	Sex	Age	IQ	Diagnosis
Treatment				
1	M	15	80	Conduct Disorder; Enuresis
2	F	18	100	Conduct Disorder; Borderline Personality
3	F	9	76	Posttraumatic Stress; Oppositional Disorder
4	M	11	96	Conduct Disorder
5	M	12	76	Attention Deficit; Conduct Disorder
6	F	18	69	Borderline Personality; Alcohol Dependency
7	M	14	96	Schizophrenia
8	M	10	110	Conduct Disorder; Attention Deficit
9	F	13	89	Borderline Personality; Conduct Disorder
10	F	18	97	Posttraumatic Stress; Conduct Disorder; Dysthymic Disorder
	5M, 5F	Avg. = 13.8	Avg. = 88.9	
Control				
1	F	15	110	Conduct Disorder; Alcohol Abuse
2	M	18	87	Schizophrenia
3	F	17	90	Conduct Disorder; Marijuana Dependence
4	F	16	100	Schizotypical
5	F	17	100	Borderline Personality; Polysubstance Abuse
6	M	13	100	Dysthymic Disorder; Oppositional Disorder
7	F	17	90	Schizophrenia, Marijuana/Alcohol Abuse
8	M	12	82	Schizophrenia
9	F	12	82	Posttraumatic Stress; Conduct Disorder
10	F	15	100	Adjustment Disorder with Mixed Emotional Features
	3M, 7F	Avg. = 15.5	Avg. = 94.1	

Source: Chamberlain and Reid 1991, p. 269.
Copyright 1991. Printed by permission from Clinical Psychology Publishing Co., Brandon, VT.

older, the Adolescent Problem Inventory (API; Gaffney & McFall 1981) was used. For those under 12, the Taxonomy of Problematic Social Situations (TPSS; Dodge, McClaskey, & Feldman 1985) was used. Both systems use the same format; the child is presented with a series of vignettes, and then is asked to role-play what his or her response would be.

All the cases in the experimental group were placed in OSLC TFC homes. The treatment included the basic components described in the previous chapters and additional psychiatric consultation and medication management as needed. In addition, program services were modified to meet the special needs of these individuals. For example, it quickly became apparent that it was necessary to provide regular crisis intervention services for this population of youngsters. In most cases, these services were provided by the child's individual therapist, and the case manager was used as a back-up. For each of the 10 experimental cases, at least one crisis occurred. In 4 of the 10 cases, crises occurred at least once per month. The substance of these crises varied, but they included suicide attempts, explosive outbursts, threats of harm to self or others, inappropriate sexual conduct, animal abuse, ingestion of nonfood substances, and running away.

Seven of the 10 control cases were placed in community settings; 3 went to residential centers, and 4 were placed in the homes of family members or relatives. The 3 remaining control cases stayed in the state hospital for the entire period of the study. The treatments provided in the control settings were varied. In the hospital and residential centers, part of the treatment was described as milieu therapy. The types of milieu treatment ranged from highly structured programs with specific behavioral targets to programs that focused on general nurturing and feedback. Some individual therapy was provided to 9 of the 10 controls. The amounts of individual treatment received ranged from an average of 77 hours for subjects in residential treatment centers to 15 hours for those who were living at home or with a relative. Group therapy was the most frequent mode of treatment for the control cases; subjects in the state hospital received an average of 156 hours, those in residential centers received 170 hours, and those living at home or with a relative received an average of 12 hours of therapy.

Hospitalization Rates

The average length of time between referral and placement out of the hospital for the two groups was examined first. TFC cases were placed in an average of 81 days (S.D. = 42); it took an average of 182 days (S.D. = 136) for control cases to be placed, and 3 of these cases were not placed in the community during the two-year span of the study. Excluding those 3 cases, and comparing the 7 control cases who were eventually placed with the 10 placed TFC cases, a reliable difference was evident between the two groups in the time from referral to community placement, favoring those in the TFC condition ($t = 4.76$; $df = 15$; $p = .01$).

Given that a child was placed in the community, the next step was to look at the amount of time he or she maintained in the placement. During the year following placement, TFC cases spent an average of 288 days (S.D. = 138) living in their communities. Three of them were rehospitalized during the first six months of their community placements. Another case was hospitalized for 10 days and then returned to her TFC home. For the 7 control cases, the average number of days spent living in the community during the year postplacement was 261 (S.D. = 157). Two were rehospitalized during the first six months, and another one was hospitalized for three days and then returned to community living. There was no difference between the two groups in terms of the rate of maintenance in their communities.

Occurrence of Problem Behaviors and Symptoms

Complete PDR data were available at all three measurement points for 7 cases in each group. At each of the three points, an average score was calculated for each child that reflected the average number of problems reported per day. As can be seen in Figure 9.3, the average daily rates for control and experimental groups were noticeably elevated at baseline, with over 20 problem behaviors reported per day. This can be compared to an average of 5 problem behaviors reported by parents of nonreferred, normal children (Chamberlain & Reid 1987). At three months postbaseline, the TFC group showed a reduction of more than 50%; the rate of reported problems for the control group showed no significant decrease. As shown in Figure 9.3, the mean for both groups dropped at seven months. These data indicate that the day-to-day prob-

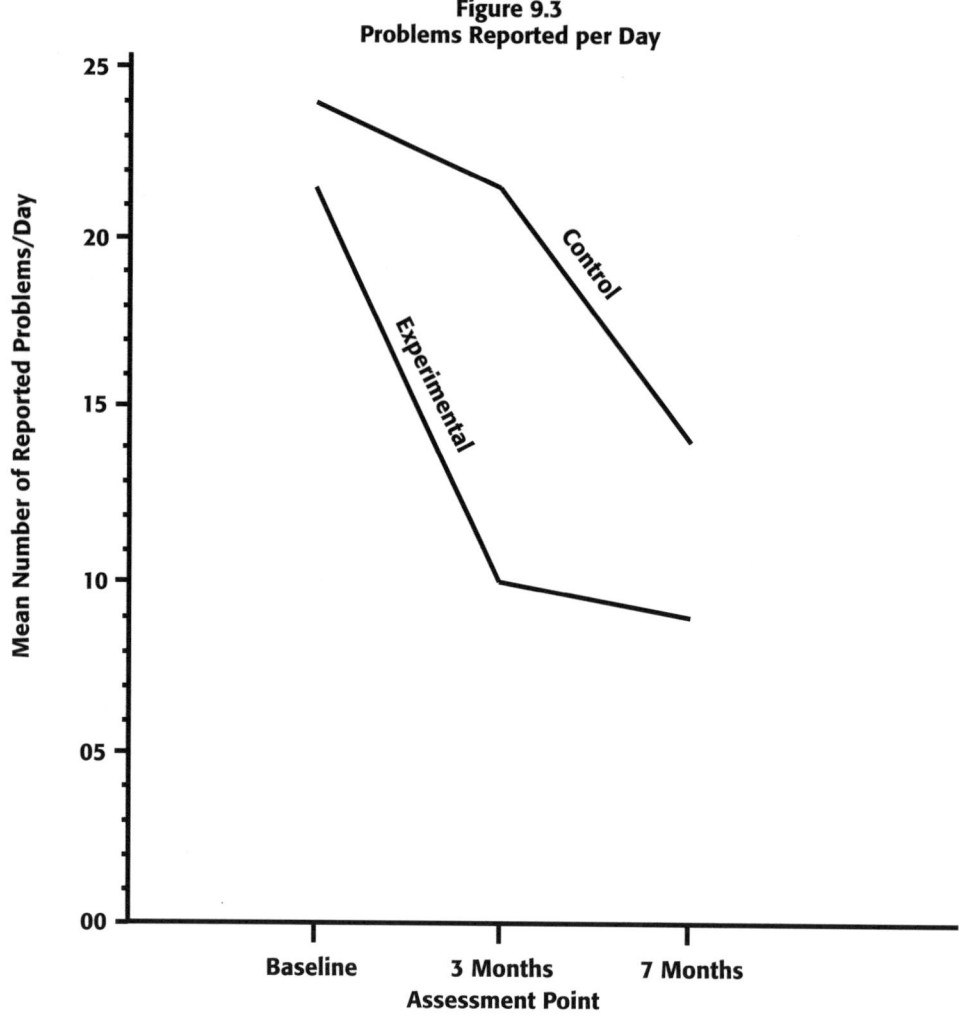

**Figure 9.3
Problems Reported per Day**

Source: Chamberlain and Reid 1991, p. 274.
Copyright 1991. Printed by permission from Clinical Psychology Publishing Co., Inc., Brandon, VT.

lems of these youngsters were not perceived by their caretakers to escalate or to be more unmanageable outside than inside the hospital. The data also suggest that being placed in a TFC setting resulted in quicker and more dramatic drops in rates of problem behaviors, as demonstrated by a significant group-by-time interaction from baseline to three months ($F[1,12] = 5.29$; $p < .05$).

The BSI data indicated that cases in both groups did not report a reduction in the presence or the severity of their symptoms from baseline to later assessments. Apparently, the children did not feel better when they were living outside the hospital. Clinically, this finding was consistent with reports of study children who said that they tended to feel less safe and secure outside the hospital.

Social Competency and Problem Solving

No improvement was observed for either group on the social competency and problem-solving measures. In fact, cases in both groups showed a (nonsignificant) decline in their scores from baseline to posttests.

SUMMARY

The two studies completed to date demonstrate that the TFC model is a viable treatment alternative for severely delinquent and disturbed children and teenagers. As has been articulated by other advocates of TFC such as Bereika (1991 – 92), Hawkins & Breiling (1989), and Bryant (1983), the TFC model has several potential advantages over more traditional group care models (these were reviewed in Chapter 1). The studies show that in terms of case outcomes, TFC compares favorably with group care. Further research is obviously needed to determine the active or necessary components of the TFC model and how these might vary for different populations of youngsters. We have recently completed one such study (Chamberlain & Reid, in press) that examines differences in risk factors and case outcomes for males and females in our TFC programs.

A fully randomized, controlled clinical trial comparing TFC to group care was recently funded by the National Institute of Mental Health, Traumatic Stress and Violent Behavior Branch. That study, Mediators of Male Delinquency (MH47458), examines the role of key social processes, such as supervision, discipline, and peer relations, to case outcomes for boys randomly assigned to TFC or to group care. The findings will help us identify the active ingredients of treatment and the factors that might inhibit or undermine treatment effects. At this point, it is clear that TFC holds great promise as a practical and effective approach for dealing with children and teenagers with severe problems.

10

METHODS OF CASE AND PROGRAM EVALUATION

In our TFC programs, as in most social service programs, we are faced with the challenge of developing inexpensive, reliable methods of case and program evaluation. The quality of information generated by our evaluation efforts largely determines our success in improving our methods and outcomes. The ongoing threats to our funding, however, make it difficult to commit program resources to assessment. As a consequence, the evaluation procedures used in our program represent a compromise between the need for high-quality data and funding constraints. Ideally, evaluation should include measures of both process and outcome.

Process measures address questions regarding the child's current functioning and changes that occur over time. This information can be used to make adjustments in almost all aspects of the program, from administration to the teenager's treatment plan. Outcome measures are typically administered at the end of treatment and during follow-up; these measures provide information on how well a particular program child and his family have done and the overall success of the intervention. Outcome measures cannot be properly interpreted without a comparison control group, however. For example, if 50% of all cases are institutionalized, is that a successful outcome? Of course, the interpretation of this result depends on the percentage of matched control cases that were institutionalized. There are several complexities involved in designating and assessing control groups that are well documented in the literature on field research (e.g., Boruch 1987; Boruch & Wothke 1985); these include ethical and political considerations in conducting random assignment in community-based (state or locally funded) programs, the issue of equivalency of treatments, and protection of confidentiality of research participants.

To conduct systematic studies using control groups, programs need consultation, experience, and sufficient funding dedicated to research. We are fortunate to be associated with the Oregon Social Learning Center, which has a long history of productive research in the areas of family interaction, children with conduct problems, and methodological issues. This association has enabled us to compete for the limited funds that are available for community program research. The studies described in Chapter 9 are the beginning of what we hope will be an ongoing programmatic effort to examine our TFC model.

THE PARENT DAILY REPORT CHECKLIST

The method of evaluation that we have found to be most cost-effective and reliable for systematic process assessments is the Parent Daily Report (PDR). The PDR is a behavioral checklist administered by telephone on a daily basis (M – F). The PDR has been examined in numerous methodological studies (e.g., Weinrott, Bauske, & Patterson 1979; Chamberlain & Reid 1987), and it has been used in treatment outcome research (e.g., Patterson 1974; Patterson & Reid 1973) and process models (e.g., Patterson, Dishion, & Chamberlain 1993). It provides feedback on the effectiveness of each child's treatment plan and helps identify which components of the Monitor Program are working and which ones need attention. The PDR makes it possible for us to obtain repeated measures of the child's progress and problems so that we can examine his or her relative adjustment over time.

The PDR was originally designed to be used in conjunction with naturalistic observations conducted by trained observers in the homes of families. The observers coded family interactions using the Family Interaction Coding System described in Reid (1978). At that time, it was hypothesized that the mechanisms that contributed to the performance of coercive behavior in children were embedded in the microsocial data generated by these observations. As the research at OSLC progressed, the focus changed from studying antisocial preschool children and their families (e.g. Patterson, Cobb, & Ray 1972) to school-age children and preteens (e.g., Reid & Patterson 1976). Gradually, it became clear that family observations were not an efficient means of studying covert antisocial problems exhibited by preteens such as stealing, lying, or fire setting. These behaviors were low baserate and rarely occurred in the home during the one-hour observation period. The PDR seemed promising as an assessment device that could reliably measure covert, low-baserate events. In the Monitor Program, PDR provides daily information on both overt and covert events that have occurred during the previous day. It is a straightforward and efficient way to collect data based on the foster parent's observations of the child.

An example of a PDR checklist is shown in Table 10.1. The checklist is administered to parents (and to TFC foster parents) during a prearranged, brief telephone call. Parents are asked to report whether each of the behaviors on the checklist has occurred during the past 24 hours. A simple response format is used (yes/no, occurred/did not occur) rather than having parents estimate the number of times a behavior occurred. It is assumed that this increases the reliability of the measure and minimizes parental bias, which has been a well-documented problem in numerous studies (e.g., Clement & Milne 1967; Schelle 1974). Most parent report measures require parents to aggregate their perceptions of their child over months or years to make ratings of behaviors or traits. Given the problems with retrospective reporting (e.g., Lewinsohn & Rosenbaum 1987), it is not surprising that global ratings by parents often show little convergence with more rigorous molecular data such as direct observations (e.g., Walters & Gilmore 1973).

Studies on Reliability and Stability

The PDR was first developed in 1969 and was administered to parents in their homes following observation sessions (Patterson 1974; Reid & Patterson 1976). Since 1974, it has been administered by telephone. Studies with clinical and nonclinical populations have shown acceptable levels of inter-interviewer reliability, ranging from 85% to 98% agreement (Jones 1974; Chamberlain & Reid 1987).

In clinical samples, a minimum of 6 calls seems to provide PDR data with adequate stability. For example, in one study the test-retest correlation for a two-week period (3 calls per week) was .60 (Patterson 1973). No differences were found in weekly levels over a four-week baseline period (12 calls; Reid &

Table 10.1
Parent Daily Report Checklist

Week of _____ Family # _____ Time of Call _____
Interviewer _____ Respondent _____

Behaviors	Mon	Tue	Wed	Thu	Fri	Sat	Sun
1. Aggressiveness							
2. Arguing							
3. Bedwetting							
4. Competitiveness							
5. Complaining							
6. Crying							
7. Defiance							
8. Destructiveness							
9. Fearfulness							
10. Fighting with siblings							
11. Fire setting							
12. Hitting others							
13. Hyperactivity							
14. Irritability							
15. Lying							
16. Negativism							
17. Noisiness							
18. Noncomplying							
19. Not eating (meals)							
20. Pants wetting							
21. Pouting							
22. Running around							
23. Running away							
24. Sadness							
25. Soiling							
26. Stealing							
27. Talking back (adult)							
28. Teasing							
29. Temper tantrums							
30. Whining							
31. Yelling							
32. Police contacts							
33. School contacts							
34. Parents hit							
35. Delinquent behavior							
Stealing?							
What?							
Where?							
When?							
36. Other							
37. Other							

Patterson 1976). A time-series analysis revealed no relationship between the length of the baseline phase and the likelihood of obtaining significant t values between phases. This suggested that 6 calls were sufficient to produce a stable estimate of the level of child problems. Using a nonclinical sample, Chamberlain and Reid (1987) collected PDR data for a four-week period (12 calls); a correlation of .82 was obtained when data from the first 6 calls were compared with data from the last 6 calls. Further analysis revealed a significant sessions effect (F[11,692] = 2.2; $p < .03$) for day one, which was greater than any other day of data collection. No differences were found between any of the other days; this indicates that the first PDR call is likely to produce an inflated estimate of child problems.

Validity of PDR

PDR scores have been compared with observational data collected in family homes in several clinical samples (e.g., Patterson 1976a; Fleischman 1981; Reid, Hinojosa-Rivero, & Lorber 1978; Forgatch & Toobert 1979). In these studies, correlations between aversive child behaviors recorded by observers and parent reports of the same behaviors on PDR have ranged from .46 to .69. Given that the two measures being compared sampled different time periods (observations, 1 hour; PDR, 24 hours) these correlations are surprisingly strong. In these same clinical studies, pre- and posttreatment changes in PDR scores were consistent with similar changes in observational scores.

CLINICAL APPLICATIONS OF PDR IN TFC PROGRAMS

Table 10.2 shows an adaptation of the PDR checklist for use with TFC foster parents. On this form, we record the occurrence of specific problem behaviors and track how many points the child has received and lost during the past 24 hours. Additional information is noted about significant events that have occurred during the previous day and details on the specific circumstances associated with point loss. We have found that the PDR provides a reliable snapshot of the child's adjustment during any given week.

This information is used in several different ways. The PDR forms for all program youths are brought each week to the foster parent meetings and the case management meetings. The information on the PDR is often used as a starting point for case discussions. Being able to systematically review the child's adjustment over a period of several days enhances the quality of the discussions about the child's treatment plan. Using PDR data, it is easy to view the child's progress or problems in the context of his or her past adjustment.

PDR data is also used to monitor cycles or patterns of behavior problems over time. For example, if a child is receiving medication for behavioral or emotional difficulties, the consulting psychiatrist uses PDR data to supplement physical examinations of the child for medication management purposes. These data can also used to keep parole or probation officers and other authorized persons informed about the current status of a particular case.

We have used PDR scores to test clinical hypotheses regarding an individual case and the entire program itself. A subset of PDR items can be used to investigate a specific question; for example, does a child's rate of aggressive behavior change after implementing a treatment plan designed to reduce aggression? Another possibility is to use the total score to examine overall trends or patterns; for example, does the child's rate of problem behaviors increase after home visits? Addition-

Table 10.2
Adapted Parent Daily Report Checklist

Week of _____ Youth _____ PDR Caller _____
Foster Parent _____ Phone # _____

Behavior	Sun	Mon	Tue	Wed	Thu	
Arguing						
Talking back						Sun/Rec. time:
Bedwetting						Unsupervised time:
Competitiveness						
Complaining						
Defiance						
Destructiveness/vandalism						Mon/Rec. time:
Encopresis						Unsupervised time:
Fighting						
Irritability						
Lying						
Negativism						
Boisterousness/rowdiness						Tue/Rec. time:
Not minding						Unsupervised time:
Staying out late						
Skipping meals						
Running away						
Swearing/obscene language						
Teasing/provoking						Wed/Rec. time:
Depression/sadness						Unsupervised time:
Sluggishness						
Jealousy						
Truancy						
Stealing						
Nervousness/jitteriness						Thu/Rec. time:
Short attention span						Unsupervised time:
Daydreaming						
Irresponsibility						
Marijuana/drug use						
Alcohol						
School problems						
TOTAL POINTS EARNED						
TOTAL POINTS LOST						
Friday	Total Points Earned		Points Lost			Recreation Time
Saturday	Total Points Earned		Points Lost			Recreation Time

Continued ...

Table 10.2 (continued from previous page)

Anything Positive/Negative Happen?	Total Recreation Time
Sunday	
Monday	
Tuesday	
Wednesday	
Thursday	

ally, PDR data can be combined across cases to study a programwide phenomenon. The following is one such example.

Do Boys and Girls Respond Differently to TFC?

The Monitor Program was originally developed for boys who were at-risk for incarceration (or reincarceration). However, once the program had been in place for about a year, we began to receive an increasing number of requests for us to develop a TFC program for girls. In 1984 we began working with girls and quickly found that they presented a new set of clinical challenges; some of these were expected, and others were not.

We had heard from other residential service providers that girls had a much higher incidence of running away than boys. We found, however, that girls did not run away more often than boys but were more *impulsive* about running away. Boys tended to run when they were doing poorly in the foster home or in school, or when they had been caught in a major misbehavior or law violation. Girls, by contrast, tended to run when they met someone who encouraged them to go; their current status or level of success in the program seemed to be unrelated.

Program completion rates for males and females were comparable: 71% of males and 73% of females who were admitted to the program successfully graduated from it. Although the program outcomes were roughly equivalent, we found that foster parents tended to become more distraught about the problems they experienced in their daily interactions with girls. In a similar vein, it was more difficult for us to find foster placements for girls. To examine this issue, we analyzed data from 88 consecutive referrals. The sample comprised 51 males and 37 females who had participated in the Monitor Program from 1984 to 1990. A detailed description of this study is provided in Chamberlain and Reid (in press). In addition to looking at the clinical profiles of these cases and their offense records, we wanted to examine the extent and topography of the daily problems that they presented while in our TFC program. Fortunately, the PDR data for these cases included this information.

For all cases, the mean rates per month (a total of 20 calls) of problem behaviors reported on PDR were summarized. The gender differences found in monthly PDR rates supported our clinical impression that females were more difficult to treat than their male counterparts. At the beginning of their placements (i.e., the first month), males showed a relatively higher rate of daily problems than females (the difference was statistically significant at $p = .04$). By the sixth month, however, females had significantly more problems, and there was a gender-by-time interaction ($p = .005$).

These data support the perception that males were improving over time while females were getting worse. This is also concordant with the frustration and sense of discouragement often expressed by foster parents and therapists working with girls. Females typically began their programs showing few problems, and as they became more comfortable and secure their level of problems increased. This pattern increased the potential that girls would be rejected in their foster homes; the foster parents felt that they were failing after making a positive start, and this feeling undermined their sense of accomplishment. Families with males experienced a steady sense of improvement over time.

It is not surprising because more females than males have been sexually abused that they may require a more intimate or long-term relationship before they feel free to act out or express their emotions. The PDR data suggest that the six-month time frame for placement and treatment that was originally developed for males may not be sufficient for female participants in our TFC program.

Examination of preprogram and postprogram arrest rates for males and females showed that overall improvement rates were comparable, however; the rates for both males and females dropped significantly from pre- to posttreatment in TFC. Other data, such as the program completion rates reported above, also showed that females had a similar likelihood of a successful outcome in TFC. The unique perspective provided by the PDR data helped us understand how day-to-day levels of problem behavior affect perceptions of treatment effectiveness. It also enabled us to identify gender-specific patterns of adjustment over time.

SUMMARY

The utility of a repeated measure, process-oriented method of data collection that can be administered to foster parents via telephone was described. Several uses for the data generated from such a measure were discussed and illustrated.

The PDR checklist has several distinct advantages: It is inexpensive, relatively reliable, and easy to administer. Programs with limited resources available for evaluation or that work with foster parents within a large geographical area should find this type of telephone-based assessment useful. In addition, the PDR checklist can be modified to fit the particular population served. For example, when studying the effects of parent-training treatment on a group of families referred for physical child abuse, Reid, Kavanagh, and Baldwin (1987) expanded the PDR to include parents' reports of the specific discipline techniques that they used during the past 24 hours, as well as ratings of how irritated they had been with their child. We have recently started to use the PDR to track the amount of time that the adolescent has spent engaging in recreational activities. This is a flexible instrument with a format that can be easily modified and expanded. We estimate that PDR takes approximately 25 minutes per week to administer, and it requires only about 30 minutes of training to become familiar with the procedures involved in collecting and recording PDR data.

APPENDIXES

***Note:** The written materials reproduced in the appendixes are provided as samples only. Before using any part of these materials, make sure the wording and intent meet all applicable local, state, and federal guidelines.*

Appendix 1: Introduction for Foster Parents: Program Values, Policies and Procedures

Welcome to the [PROGRAM NAME] team. This notebook provides an overview of program values, policies, and procedures. Please read it carefully. We invite your questions and comments. Feel free to contact [NAME], program director, or [NAME], case manager, at [PHONE #] with any concerns. Keep this notebook handy so you can refer to it as questions come up during the placement.

PROGRAM VALUES

The overriding ethic in our program is a belief in the possibility of positive change. The following program values are the guiding principles under which we operate.

Values on Working with Treatment Foster Parents

Treatment foster parents are the primary therapeutic and socializing agents for the youths in our program, and we strive to establish and maintain a collaborative and supportive relationship with them.

Treatment foster parents are teachers for the youths placed with them.

The central role and daily influence of the treatment foster parents on the child are a key aspect of the child's treatment plan.

Treatment foster parents are given all of the information available on a case before a placement is made and are encouraged to ask questions and seek further details before making a decision to accept a program child.

We believe in the treatment foster parent's potential to implement specific behavior management skills that will help the child achieve treatment goals.

We respect the integrity of the program's treatment foster families, including their schedules and demands of daily life.

We strive to continuously include the treatment foster parent's concerns and input into the child's treatment plan.

We build on the strengths of treatment foster parents and provide constructive feedback to help them improve their therapeutic effectiveness.

Values on Working with the Program Child's Family

Our program recognizes the potential of the child's natural family to provide guidance and support for their child's positive adjustment.

We respect the child's relationship with his family and whenever possible attempt to support and promote it.

We are committed to enhancing the positive potential of family relationships.

Disrupted family relationships are a significant problem for program youth. Even when a child's family is unable to meet his socioemotional needs, it is still desirable and therapeutic to help the child build a constructive relationship with his family.

We attempt to avoid any roadblocks to communication with the child's family members. Members of our staff are available to family members at all times for questions, consultation, and support.

We believe that families can change areas that are problematic for them, and we are committed to helping them reach positive goals.

We recognize that parents are in a difficult situation when their child is removed from their home.

Whenever feasible, we try to reunite children in a timely fashion with their families.

Once the child has completed the foster care program and is returned to his home, we are dedicated to providing services and support to help the child succeed at home and in his community.

Values on Working with the Teenager

We are committed to providing the youth with a well-supervised, humane, predictable, and safe living environment.

We work hard to help the teenager change problems and behaviors that interfere with success at home, at school, and in the community.

We believe that the best way to change behavior is to reinforce the adolescent's strengths and recognize his efforts.

We think that consequences for negative behavior should be immediate, well-specified, brief, and delivered without anger or violence.

We attempt to separate the teenager from negative peers and help him develop new skills, including recreational interests and hobbies.

Program teenagers are involved in planned treatment sessions and have continuous access to staff.

POLICIES AND PROCEDURES

Communications

Parole or Probation Officer. The assigned parole or probation officer will meet with the child on a regular basis. These meetings are scheduled by the child's case manager and usually occur at [PLACE]. Additional meetings may be scheduled, as needed. The case manager maintains routine contact with the parole or probation officer regarding each child. All communication with the parole or probation officer should go through the case manager.

Our Staff. Our treatment program uses a team approach. All major decisions regarding a child should be discussed with the case manager, the therapist, and the foster parents. This may sound cumbersome, but it allows us to make thoughtful case planning decisions, even in difficult situations.

On weekdays, you will be called for Parent Daily Report (PDR) data. These calls generally occur in the morning before 11:00 a.m.; each parent is assigned a specific time to be available for the call.

On weekends, a senior staff member is on call. At the beginning of each month, you will be given the on-call schedule listing the name and phone number of the person on call for each weekend. If you are unable to reach the on-call person, call other staff members on the list until you reach someone. Try to stay out of the position of making unilateral decisions in emergency situations. Unilateral decisions are not in keeping with the team approach and are not consistent with program policy. Perhaps the most important thing to keep in mind is *when in doubt, call.*

Parents or Relatives of Your Foster Child. All home visits must be arranged by the case manager, who will take care of scheduling, coordinate transportation, and notify parole or probation personnel. The child's parents or relatives are given a sheet that explains the rules for home visits. You will be given a copy of this.

The program child must obtain your permission in advance before making telephone calls to his parents or relatives. Because family relationships are often a sensitive area, the plan for telephone contact between your program child and his natural family will be discussed and monitored during our weekly meetings. *Drop-in visits by family members are strictly against program rules.* If this occurs, call the [PROGRAM NAME] or the on-call staff member immediately.

Children's Services Division Certifiers. Before a child is placed in your home, you will be visited by the CSD certifier. [STAFF MEMBER'S NAME] will answer your questions about this process. You will be recertified by CSD on an annual basis.

Drug And Alcohol Monitoring

Room Searches. Periodically, you will be asked to conduct room searches. If possible, do this when the child is not home. The purpose is not to be secretive (program children are notified that routine room searches are conducted) but rather to avoid confrontation or undue discomfort on the child's part. Look thoroughly through clothing pockets, drawers, closets, under mattresses, in light fixtures, and anywhere else in the room that might be a good hiding place. If unauthorized items are found, contact the case manager or the on-call staff member immediately.

Urinalysis. Urinalysis will be conducted routinely for all children at least monthly. Additional tests will be requested if drug or alcohol use is suspected. You will be given a supply of jars. When you do a test, there are several steps to follow:

1. If at all possible, witness the taking of the sample. This prevents substituting clean urine or other substances.

2. Label the jar with the child's name and the date.

3. Keep the jar in your possession until you turn it in to us. Don't worry too much about the sample deteriorating. It will last for two days if kept refrigerated.

Your Alcohol. If you have liquor in the house, know exactly how much you have at all times. It is a good idea to keep any hard liquor locked up. Do a daily count of beer in the refrigerator.

Confidentiality

It is important to protect the privacy of the children in our program. With this in mind, you should refrain from disclosing case information to friends or others who do not need to know the details of the child's history or current problems. You will be required to sign a Confidentiality Agreement form. This is a requirement for all [PROGRAM NAME] staff.

Protecting Yourself

To avoid accusations and subsequent investigations regarding alleged sexual misconduct on the part of foster parents toward children in the program, it is the policy of this program that you will avoid circumstances that could invite such allegations. Foster parents should not be in a closed bedroom alone with foster children of the opposite sex at any time. Inappropriate physical contact or contact that could be construed as inappropriate should be strictly avoided.

Church

Church attendance may be invited but must never be required. If a child in your home expresses an interest in a certain denomination, please inform the case manager at once. All further contact must be approved by the youth's parents.

Respite Care

We encourage foster parents to take occasional breaks. Notify the case manager if you would like respite. A two-week advance notice is best. All children in the program are foster children, and they must reside in a home that has been certified by CSD. If you want to leave the child with another adult, remember, no matter what period of time the child will be absent from your home, the program staff *must be notified* of any absence. Program approval must be given before the child can be placed with someone other than [PROGRAM NAME] foster parents.

Parole or Probation Regulations

The children in this program are either on parole from [NAME OF INSTITUTION] or on probation status. They have met with their parole officers and are bound to abide by the parole agreement established for them. As program staff and foster parents, we are also bound to abide by the terms of that agreement. Please read it carefully.

Firearms

Because the children involved in this program are on parole or probation, it is our policy that any firearms in the home must be kept unloaded and secured by a locking door that requires a key or combination to open. The ammunition must be stored in a separate location. This procedure follows the guidelines set forth by CSD.

Keys

Keys to motor vehicles, firearm cabinets, and storage areas for valuables and prescription drugs must be kept secure and inaccessible to children in the program. All keys should be kept on your person or in a locked cabinet at all times.

Medication

Prescription drugs should be kept in a locked cabinet. Individual tablets and capsules should be counted and their number recorded on a regular basis. Medication intended for children in the program should be administered on a dose-by-dose basis.

Compensation

We realize that no amount of money can adequately compensate a family for the time and emotional investment that is required to take care of a troubled foster child.

The [PROGRAM NAME] parents are compensated at a rate of [AMOUNT] per child per month. In addition, a $60 clothing and incidentals allowance is provided for the upcoming month, making a total compensation of [AMOUNT]. Allowance money for the child, as well as cigarette purchases, come out of the [AMOUNT]. If a child enters or graduates from your home during the month, compensation and clothing allowance will be prorated to reflect the actual days that the child was in your home.

When staff and foster parents agree that a respite is necessary and the foster child spends the weekend at another home, or the child goes on a home visit, the foster parents receive compensation as usual for those days. When foster parents go on vacation without the foster child, they are not paid for those days.

If a child runs away, foster parents will be compensated for 14 additional days from the date of the child's departure. If the child is returned to your home or another child is placed in your home during that time, compensation will continue as usual. If a child is not placed in your home, compensation will stop.

Finally, increases in compensation are based on several criteria: daily Parent Daily Report calls, making appointments on time, attending weekly foster parent meetings, seniority, success rate, and program budget limitations.

Discipline

Although the children in this program often require firm limits, physical discipline is never appropriate and should not be used. Typical methods of disciplining children include work chores, removal of privileges, demotion to a lower program level, or time out. An individualized plan will be developed for you to implement with the program child placed in your home. In the extremely rare instance in which a child presents a clear and present danger to others, the following steps should be taken immediately:

1. Contact the on-call staff member.
2. Call 911 for assistance.

Mail Policy

Because we contract with the state and serve children who are committed to the training schools, we have adopted their procedures for screening mail.

Incoming Mail. Mail that is *not* from an elected official, CSD, or an attorney shall be opened and inspected for the purpose of intercepting contraband. Contraband found in incoming mail will be removed, "contraband removed" will be written on the envelope, and the legitimate contents will then be forwarded to the child.

Outgoing Mail. The program child is allowed to send sealed mail to any elected official, court, CSD, or attorney.

Prohibited Mail. Prohibited mail includes both incoming and outgoing mail that:

1. Contains threats of physical harm to any person or threats of criminal activity
2. Threatens blackmail or extortion
3. Concerns the sending of contraband
4. Concerns plans of escape
5. Concerns plans for activities in violation of program rules
6. Concerns plans for criminal activity
7. Is in code
8. Contains information that, if communicated, would create a clear and present danger of violence and physical harm to another person or of destruction of property
9. Contains sexually explicit material that, in terms of the emotional maturity of the child, is presented in such a manner that program staff consider it to be injurious to the welfare of the child
10. Contains contraband material
11. Is from inmates (other than family members) in institutions or programs operated by the Corrections Division

Prohibited mail will be handled in the following manner:

Outgoing mail. Program staff may disapprove any mail if its contents fall into any of the above categories in whole or significant part.

Incoming mail. Program staff may disapprove mail for receipt by the child if its contents fall into any one or more of the above categories in whole or significant part. However, if the only violation is that it contains contraband that can be disposed of, the mail shall be delivered to the child after the contraband is removed.

Handling Disapproved Mail. If program staff determine that mail which has been sent to a child is in violation of the rules stated here and may not be delivered, it will be returned to the sender along with written notice of that determination and the reason for disapproval within seven days of the action.

If these rules are violated repeatedly, all of the child's mail will be forwarded through our program.

Appendix 2: Agreement Between the Foster Parents and the Program

JOB DESCRIPTION FOR FULL-TIME FOSTER PARENTS

Summary of Duties

Foster parents are responsible for the care and supervision of one foster child, and it is their duty to implement and monitor the treatment plan that has been developed for that child. Further, foster parents are required to support and cooperate with ongoing program planning and activities. Foster parents are expected to follow program policies and direct any inquiries regarding the child or the child's family to the program staff. Foster parents will be supervised by the program director and/or case manager.

Qualifications

Foster parents must have the following qualifications:

1. A certified foster home
2. A car and a current driver's license
3. An interest and ability to work with hard-to-reach youth on a full-time basis
4. Completion of the [PROGRAM NAME] training sessions and a willingness to continue training on an ongoing basis, as provided by program staff

Duties

Professional foster parents are expected to:
A. Participate in training sessions
B. Provide basic care and supervision for the child, including
   1. Room and board
   2. Nurturance, acceptance in the family
   3. Clear and fair limits and rules; consistency
   4. Clothing

5. Transportation
6. Medical and dental care
C. Work as an integral part of the child's treatment team
   1. Cooperate with program staff to provide a smooth transition for the child when he is admitted into or is discharged from the foster home
   2. Work with program staff to set up an individualized point chart that fits the daily schedule of the child
   3. Observe the child's behavior and implement the point program by conducting a daily review of the child's progress with the child
   4. Provide constant supervision on Level 1; implement planning and approval procedures at all times on Levels 2 and 3
   5. Keep program staff informed of all significant events and developments on a daily basis
   6. Work with program staff and other personnel as follows:
      a. Provide point chart and level progress reports
      b. Cooperate with parole or probation officer visits
      c. Work closely with program staff at all times
      d. Make arrangements to be available at designated time for Parent Daily Report calls
   7. Call program staff when necessary
D. Work with the community
   1. Register the child in school
   2. Participate in parent – teacher conferences
   3. Keep program staff informed of the child's progress in school, present program in a positive manner in contacts with school personnel
   4. Foster and encourage community involvement
   5. Maintain professional status with community when discussing program or child, always adhering to the confidentiality agreement regarding both the child and the child's family
E. Work with the child's natural parents
   1. Cooperate with home visit and aftercare plans for each child
   2. Provide support and encouragement to the child about those plans
   3. Maintain professional standards with the child and parents by being positive about plans, visits, and support
   4. Direct any difficulties to program staff, never to the child, parents, or community
F. Notify the program of emergencies
   1. Child running away
   2. Accidents
   3. Medical problems
   4. Any family or personal emergency that would cause distress
G. Notify the program when
   1. The child does not return at the planned time from an activity
   2. Foster parents have a new phone number or plan to move
   3. The child will be taken out of the city or state or will be gone overnight with foster parents or anyone else

4. There is a change in household membership
5. The child goes on a school trip, church outing, etc.

AGREEMENT

Agreement made this ___ day of _____, 19__ by and between [PROGRAM NAME] of [ADDRESS] hereinafter referred to as [PROGRAM NAME] and [FOSTER PARENTS' NAMES] of [ADDRESS] hereinafter referred to as Treatment Parent(s).

In consideration of the mutual promises contained in this Agreement, the parties agree as follows:

Services

The Treatment Parent(s) agree(s) to provide full-time care and supervision for one (1) youth participating in [PROGRAM NAME] to be placed in the household of the Treatment Parent(s), and to implement and monitor the youth's treatment plan as prescribed by [PROGRAM NAME] staff.

As the key agent(s) of support and change for the youth in his/her/their care, the Treatment Parent(s) agree(s) to undergo initial intensive training, provided by [PROGRAM NAME] staff members, prior to placement of the youth. The Treatment Parent(s) further agree(s) to attend weekly meetings with [PROGRAM NAME] staff to discuss the progress of the youth in his/her/their care, to receive ongoing training, and to receive instructions and directions concerning the treatment of the youth. Furthermore, the Treatment Parent(s) agree(s) to provide daily telephone reports with [PROGRAM NAME] staff Monday through Friday of each week.

The Treatment Parent(s) understand(s) that intensive supervision is an important aspect of the child's treatment plan and agree(s) to exercise such supervision, which includes knowing where the child is at all times.

All overnight absences of the youth from the Treatment Parent(s) shall be approved by [PROGRAM NAME] staff in advance. All overnight absences from the home of the Treatment Parent(s), even if accompanied by the Treatment Parent(s), shall be approved by [PROGRAM NAME] staff in advance. All visits by the youth with his or her natural parents or other relatives must be arranged through [PROGRAM NAME] staff.

[PROGRAM NAME] agrees to provide support and assistance to the Treatment Parent(s) at all times. During office hours, such help will be available through [PROGRAM NAME]'s office; an on-call list of program staff members will be provided by [PROGRAM NAME] to the Treatment Parent(s) for use during non-office hours.

The Treatment Parent(s) agree(s) to maintain a valid driver's license and availability of a car in good working condition. He/she/they also agree(s) to maintain telephone service to his/her/their residence.

Compensation

[PROGRAM NAME] agrees to provide compensation to the Treatment Parent(s) in the amount of $_____ per month. This monthly amount will be prorated if placement or termination of placement occurs during the month, rather than at the beginning or end of a month. If, during the course of a month, the youth does not reside in the household of the Treatment Parent(s) for reasons of a home visit, detention of ten (10) days or less, authorized leave, or a runaway of ten (10) days or less, the compensation will be continued during these absences.

Baserate compensations to the Treatment Parent(s) are made for the purpose of covering the expenses incurred for regular upkeep of the youth placed in his/her/their home, such as food, housing, utilities, transportation, allowances, entertainment, etc. Reimbursements are not intended as compensation for time and effort by the Treatment Parent(s). Because of the nature of the contractual relationship between the Treatment Parent(s) and [PROGRAM NAME], no benefits, including unemployment insurance, are provided under this agreement.

Increases in compensation amounts may be awarded by [PROGRAM NAME] staff based on increases in expenses, budget considerations, and other relevant factors.

Finally, [PROGRAM NAME] agrees to provide the Treatment Parent(s) with a monthly allowance to buy clothes for the youth in his/her/their care and cover other incidental expenses incurred in caring for the youth. Allowance money and/or money for cigarette purchases and normal expenses of youth upkeep are not considered incidental expenses.

Payment of all compensation amounts due to the Treatment Parent(s) according to the stipulations above will take place on the last working day of the service month.

Insurance and Liability

The Treatment Parent(s) understand(s) and agree(s) that [PROGRAM NAME] does not provide insurance against risks associated with placement of the youth in his/her/their household. It is further understood and agreed that [PROGRAM NAME] will not be held responsible or liable for any loss, damage, or injury resulting from placement of the youth in the home of the Treatment Parent(s). The Treatment Parent(s) agree(s) to purchase and maintain adequate insurance coverage to protect himself/herself/themselves against reasonable risks to home, car, and other possessions, as well as to his/her/their person(s), created by the presence of the youth in his/her/their household.

INITIATION AND TERMINATION OF THIS AGREEMENT

This agreement becomes effective on the date the youth is placed in the home or on the date the Treatment Parent(s) begin(s) the training described in the second paragraph under the section entitled "Services" of this document, whichever is later.

This agreement will terminate at the time the placement of the youth is terminated.

Treatment Parent(s): _____
                                              Date

_____
       Date

Address _____

**For
[PROGRAM NAME]** _____ **Date**

[PERSON'S NAME]
Program Director

LIABILITY COVERAGE FOR FOSTER PARENTS

As a certified foster parent, it is important for you to be aware of the following information regarding liability coverage through the state's liability fund for the willful and malicious acts of foster children placed in your home.

The Children's Services Division may be found liable for damages by such child to other persons or to property, subject to each of the following conditions, which shall apply to each claim:

1. The child is residing in a foster home certified by the Children's Services Division under the provisions of [STATUTE], even though the child may be temporarily absent from such home, but is not residing elsewhere with approval of the division;

2. The damages were in fact done wholly or partly by such child acting singly or in concert with other persons and were done by such child intentionally or willfully and maliciously; and

3. The damages are not attributable to any adult in a manner or to a degree that would, in the opinion of the Department of Justice or a court of competent jurisdiction, reasonably relieve the child of blame.

The following are not covered and, therefore, cannot be reimbursed:

1. Any losses arising out of theft by a foster child.

2. Bodily injury and property damage claims arising out of the operation of a motor vehicle by a foster child.

Note: Please be sure not to leave car keys in automobiles, as this is a temptation for the child to use the car without permission of the owner.

Filing a Claim

To ensure the processing of your claim, these procedures are to be followed:

1. Claims must be filed within 180 days from the date of occurrence [STATUTE]. [SPECIFY FORM TO BE USED].

2. *If possible, all claim forms should be accompanied by bills, estimates, receipts, canceled checks, or proof of purchase.*

3. Describe all damaged property in detail (if necessary, on a separate page), i.e., age, type of material or construction, where purchased, etc. Include photographs, if possible.

If you have any questions regarding the claims procedure or what losses will be covered, please call the Risk Management Division, Claims Section.

[PROGRAM NAME]

OVERVIEW OF PROGRAM POLICIES AND PROCEDURES FOR THE CHILD'S NATURAL PARENTS

During their first three weeks in the program, children are allowed to make one phone call to either their parent(s) or an approved individual (relative, guardian, sibling, etc.). They are permitted to receive letters during this three-week period.

Once a program child reaches Level 2 (after three weeks), he is encouraged to go for home visits or outings with his parent(s) or approved individual(s), provided that three conditions are met:

1. The child must have earned the required number of points during the past week.

2. The parent(s) or approved individual(s) must arrange the time and date of the visit at least *three* working days in advance of the visit.

3. The parent(s) or approved individual(s) agree to provide close supervision of the youth during the home visit or outing.

Please contact your child's case manager about the proposed visits, *not* the foster home where the youth is staying. Your child's case manager is:

_____   _____
     Case Manager   **Phone Numbers**

Please do not buy your child any clothing, toys, books, or other items without prior approval from the program. Although it is fine to buy your child special treats during the visit, please do not send any of these items back with him. Any toys, clothes, tapes, or items of food sent back with the child without prior approval will be confiscated and returned to you.

If you have any questions about the procedures described above, feel free to contact us.

[PROGRAM NAME]
PARENT GRIEVANCE PROCEDURES

Program foster parents are granted the same rights as regular employees of [PROGRAM NAME] with regard to grievance procedures; such rights become available after the completion of a three-month probationary period — the same period required of regular staff.

The steps involved in the grievance procedures are as follows:

1. A foster parent is expected to consult first with the project manager or project director regarding any action, either expressed or implied, that is experienced as unfair or inequitable. If such consultation does not produce satisfactory resolution of the problem, the employee should submit a letter of complaint to the Staff Council requesting a hearing on the matter.

2. The Staff Council will hear and review all evidence presented by the grievant(s) and the [PROGRAM NAME] staff. After consideration, a written recommendation for action will be submitted to the Management Committee, which will issue a decision on the matter within 15 calendar days of receipt of the original complaint.

3. If action by the Staff Council and Management Committee is not satisfactory to either party, an appeal may be made in writing to the chairman of the Board of Directors for a hearing before the Board. The decision of the Board will be made in as timely a fashion as possible, and will be final. If such an appeal is made, it must be submitted in writing within 30 days of the Management Committee decision.

[PROGRAM NAME]

PROCEDURE FOR REPORTING UNAUTHORIZED DEPARTURES

1. Call the case manager or other [PROGRAM NAME] staff at [PHONE #].
2. Go immediately to the Eugene Police Department located in City Hall at [PLACE].
3. Tell the officer that the youth has an "unauthorized departure" from the [PROGRAM NAME].
4. The police will ask for the youth's full name and birthdate, and a physical description of the clothes the youth was wearing when last seen.
5. They will ask for the foster parent's name, address, birthdate, and relationship to the youth.
6. They will also ask for a contact person. Please give them [STAFF MEMBER'S NAME] name and telephone number, as well as your own. It would be a good idea to give them the youth's case manager's number and his parole officer's number as well.

HANDOUT FOR PROGRAM YOUTHS

Youth Rights

Aside from the basics of care, supervision, shelter, and food, you have the following rights:

1. The right to not be discriminated against because of race, color, creed, or sexual preference
2. The right to call your attorney
3. The right to call your therapist
4. The right to file a grievance should you feel you are treated unfairly

Before filing a grievance, you are encouraged to negotiate for the changes that you want. Steps for negotiation are as follows:

1. Talk to your foster parents and therapist about the change you want.
2. Negotiate a plan for change.
3. Identify the things that indicate success.
4. Identify consequences for success and failure.
5. If this fails and you are still dissatisfied, repeat steps 1 – 4 with your case manager.
6. If you cannot reach an agreement with your case manager, you may file a grievance.

The steps for filing a grievance are as follows:

1. Notify the program director, [NAME] [PHONE #].
2. Within three days, a meeting will be scheduled with you and the other people concerned (for example, your foster parents, your therapist, and your parole or probation officer).
3. You will receive a written summary of the outcome of the grievance.

Good luck in the program. Remember, over 75% of the youths who start these programs finish them.

HANDOUT FOR FOSTER PARENTS AND PROGRAM STAFF

Youth Rights

The youths who participate in the [PROGRAM NAME] have the following basic rights:

1. They may contact their attorney at any time.
2. They may contact their program therapist at any time.
3. Information about their past difficulties is confidential and should not be discussed with those who do not have a need to know.
4. They may file a grievance with the program director, and an appointment will be set up within three days with all parties concerned (e.g., foster parents, therapist, parole or probation officer, case manager, etc.).

Beyond these rights, youths are encouraged to suggest and negotiate to make changes in their programs. This is done by contacting their therapist or case manager. Foster parents will routinely be included in these negotiations.

INITIAL CHECKLIST FOR FOSTER PARENTS

Clothing Inventory

		#
A.	**Jacket (warm weather/cold weather)**	
	Condition	
B.	**Jeans/Pants**	
	Condition	
C.	**Shirts/Blouses**	
	Condition	
D.	**Shoes**	
	Condition	
E.	**Underclothes**	
	Condition	
F.	**Bathrobe**	
	Condition	

Appointment with [STAFF MEMBER'S NAME] to determine needs

Clothing purchased, receipts given to [STAFF MEMBER'S NAME]

MEDICAL INFORMATION SHEET FOR FOSTER PARENTS

Once a program youth has been placed in your home, it is your responsibility to make sure he is provided with medical attention. Please contact [STAFF MEMBER'S NAME] regarding a medical card, and make appointments with a medical doctor and a dentist within the first three weeks of placement. Please use this form to assist us in tracking the medical care the child has received.

Dr. _____ Phone _____

Address _____

Initial appt. _____ Follow-up _____

Medical needs (if any) _____

Medication _____

Directions for use _____

Length of prescription _____

Dentist _____ Phone _____

Address _____

Initial appt. _____ Follow-up _____

Dental needs _____

Appendix 3: Parental and Youth Consent Forms for Participation in the Program

PARENTAL CONSENT FORM

I have read the explanation of the [PROGRAM NAME].

I understand that my youth and I will be participating in the [PROGRAM NAME] at [NAME OF ORGANIZATION], which is under the direction of [DIRECTOR'S NAME].

I willingly give my permission to participate and for my youth to participate in the project, knowing that any information gathered about my family and my youth from court, police, school, Children's Services Division, public agencies, personal interviews, telephone interviews, and questionnaires will be kept strictly confidential. I give authorization for the above-named agencies to share and exchange information with the staff of [PROGRAM NAME] at [NAME OF ORGANIZATION].

I understand that no one outside [NAME OF ORGANIZATION] will have access to individual records without my prior written consent.

I understand that my youth or I have the right to withdraw from this program at any time.

I understand the potential risks and benefits involved in our participation in the program.

I have read the information above concerning the [PROGRAM NAME] at [NAME OF ORGANIZATION] and have had all my questions about the program and my and my youth's participation answered to my satisfaction. Thus, I hereby give my consent to participate in the [PROGRAM NAME] at [NAME OF ORGANIZATION].

_____   _____
      Mother   **Witness**

_____   _____
      Father   **Date**

YOUTH CONSENT FORM

I have read the Parental Consent form. I understand the conditions that my parents have agreed to for my participation in the [PROGRAM NAME] at [NAME OF ORGANIZATION], and I also agree to these conditions.

_____   _____
Youth   **Witness**

_____
Date

APPENDIX 4: PROGRAM OVERVIEW

The [PROGRAM NAME] is designed to provide a community-based treatment alternative to institutionalization for males from 12 to 18 years old who have a history of law violations. These youth typically have a history of multiple and chronic adjustment problems: school failure, inappropriate family interactions, aggression, drug and alcohol use, poor peer relations, inadequate coping and social skills, minimal work skills, and low self-esteem. The [PROGRAM NAME] is a six-month placement for youths who have been committed or are at-risk for commitment to juvenile detention facilities.

The youths are placed with CSD-certified foster parents who are recruited by program staff. Program staff and foster parents work together to develop and implement individualized treatment programs for each youth. One youth is placed in each home. The program takes advantage of the natural parenting abilities of the treatment foster parents, their stable and nurturing family relations, and research-based treatment methods that have been developed for antisocial youth. Family members are encouraged to contact the child's case manager to obtain progress reports and arrange home visits. Individual and family therapy are provided for all program youths. Program staff coordinate services for youths with schools, at work, with the parole or probation office, and in special interest areas to ensure an integrated approach.

The [PROGRAM NAME] focuses on helping the youth's natural family or aftercare placement family reintegrate the youth after the placement period to ensure that the youth continues to make progress in areas where positive behavior changes have been achieved during the placement. Program staff continue to work with the reunified families for 12 months after youths leave foster care.

The assumptions of the program are twofold: first, that the conduct of these youngsters can be altered by changing the circumstances that influence them; and second, that their natural or aftercare placement families can learn to support positive social behaviors so they will be accepted in the community, reducing the likelihood of institutionalization. The [PROGRAM NAME] has been operating since [DATE] and receives referrals from the state juvenile courts, attorneys, parole officers, and CSD caseworkers.

The [PROGRAM NAME] is one of 13 statewide diversion programs funded by [SOURCE].

For further information, contact the director, [NAME], or the case manager, [NAME], at [PHONE #].

Appendix 4:
Program Overview

References

Ageton, S. S. The dynamics of female delinquency, 1976–1980. *Criminology,* 1983, *21*(4), 555–584.

Bank, L., Chamberlain, P., & Ray, J. *A study of the incidence of violence in chronic juvenile offenders: Implications for treatment,* in preparation.

Bank, L., Marlowe, J. H., Reid, J. B., Patterson, G. R., & Weinrott, M. R. A comparative evaluation of parent training interventions for families of chronic delinquents. *Journal of Abnormal Child Psychology,* 1991, *19*(1), 15–33.

Becker, W. C., Madsen, C. H., Arnold, C. R., & Thomas, D. R. The contingent use of teacher attention and praise in reducing classroom behavior problems. *Journal of Special Education,* 1967, *1,* 287-307.

Beljaars, I. C. M., & Berger, M. A. The coaching project: Training by nonprofessionals for youths with poor community living skills. In P. M. G. Emmelkamp, W. T. A. M. Everaerd, F. Viraaimaat, & M. J. M. van Son (Eds.), *Advances in theory and practice in behavior therapy.* Amsterdam: Swets & Zeitlinger, 1988.

Bereika, G. M. Individualized residential treatment: An alternative to acute psychiatric hospitalization. *Foster Family–Based Treatment Association Newsletter,* winter 1991–92, *2*(3).

Berger, R. J. Female delinquency in the emancipation era: A review of the literature. *Sex Roles,* 1989, *21*(5/6), 375–399.

Boruch, R. F. Conducting social experiments. In D. S. Cordray, H. S. Bloom, & R. J. Light (Eds.), *Evaluation practice in review: New directions for program evaluation* (No. 34). San Francisco: Jossey-Bass, 1987.

Boruch, R. F., & Wothke, W. Seven kinds of randomization plans for designing field experiments. In R. F. Boruch & W. Wothke (Eds.), *Randomization and field experimentation: New directions for program evaluation* (No. 28). San Francisco: Jossey-Bass, 1985.

Bryant, B. Special foster care: A history and rationale. *Journal of Clinical Child Psychology,* 1980, *10*(1), 8–20.

Bryant, B. *Special foster care: A history and rationale.* Verone, VA: People Places, Inc, 1983.

Capaldi, D. M. Co-occurrence of conduct problems and depressive symptoms in early adolescent boys: I. Familial factors and general adjustment at Grade 6. *Development and Psychopathology,* 1991, *3,* 277-300.

Capaldi, D. M., & Patterson, G. R. The relation of parental transitions to boys' adjustment problems: I. A linear hypothesis, and II. Mothers at risk for transitions and unskilled parenting. *Developmental Psychology,* 1991, *27,* 489–504.

Caspi, A., Elder, G. H., & Bem, D. J. Moving against the world: Life course patterns of explosive children. *Developmental Psychology,* 1987, *23,* 308–313.

Cautley, P. W., & Aldridge, M. J. Predicting success for new foster parents. *Social Work,* 1975, *4*(2), 48–53.

Chamberlain, P. Comparative evaluation of specialized foster care for seriously delinquent youths: A first step. *Community Alternatives: International Journal of Family Care,* 1990, *2,* 21–36.

Chamberlain, P., & Antoine, K. *Curriculum for parent groups,* in preparation.

Chamberlain, P., & Patterson, G. R. Aggressive behavior in middle childhood. In D. Shaffer, A. A. Ehrhardt, & L. L. Greenhill (Eds.), *The clinical guide to child psychiatry* (pp. 229–250). New York: The Free Press, 1984.

Chamberlain, P., Patterson, G. R., Reid, J. B., Forgatch, M. S., & Kavanagh, K. Observation of client resistance. *Behavior Therapy,* 1984, *15,* 144–155.

Chamberlain, P., & Ray, J. The therapy process code: A multidimensional system for observing therapist and client interactions in family treatment. In R. J. Prinz (Ed.), *Advances in behavioral assessment of children and families* (Vol. 4, pp. 189–217). Greenwich, CT: JAI Press, 1988.

Chamberlain, P., & Reid, J. B. Parent observation and report of child symptoms. *Behavioral Assessment,* 1987, *2,* 97–109.

Chamberlain, P., & Reid, J. B. Using a specialized foster care community treatment model for children and adolescents leaving the state mental hospital. *Journal of Community Psychology,* 1991, *19,* 266–276.

Chamberlain, P., & Reid, J. B. *Differences in risk factors and adjustment for male and female delinquents in treatment foster care,* in press.

Chesney-Lind, M. Girls in jail. *Crime and Delinquency,* 1988, *34*(2), 150–168.

Clement, P. W., & Milne, P. C. Group play therapy and tangible reinforcers used to modify the behavior of 8-year-old boys. *Behavior Research and Therapy,* 1967, *5,* 301–312.

Coddington, R. The significance of life events as etiological factors in the disease of children: The study of the normal population. *Journal of Psychosomatic Research,* 1972, *16,* 205–213.

Coie, J. D., & Kupersmidt, J. B. A behavioral analysis of emerging social status in boys' groups. *Child Development,* 1983, *54,* 1400–1416.

Dennis, K. W. STAR–Specialized team for AIDS relief: A therapeutic foster care program for children with AIDS. *Community Alternatives International Journal of Family Care,* 1992, *4*(2), 269–280.

Derogatis, L. R., & Spencer, P. M. *The Brief Symptom Inventory (BSI) administration, scoring, & procedures manual–I.* Baltimore, MD: Clinical Psychometric Research, 1982.

Dodge, K. A., McClaskey, C. L., & Feldman, E. L. A situational approach to the assessment of social competence in children.

Journal of Consulting and Clinical Psychology, 1985, *53,* 344–353.

Elder, G. H., Caspi, A., & Downey, G. Problem behavior in family relationships: A multigenerational analysis. In A. Sorensen, F. Weinert, & L. Sherrod (Eds.), *Human development: Interdisciplinary perspective* (pp. 92–118). Hillsdale, NJ: Lawrence Erlbaum Associates, 1983.

Elliott, D. S., Huizinga, D., & Ageton, S. S. *Explaining delinquency and drug use.* Beverly Hills, CA: Sage, 1985.

Farrington, D. P. The family background of aggressive youths. In L. Hersov, M. Berger, & D. Shaffer (Eds.), *Aggression and antisocial behavior in childhood and adolescence* (pp. 73–93). Elmsford, NY: Pergamon, 1978.

Felner, R., Farber, S., & Primavera, J. In R. D. Felner, L. A. Jason, J. N. Moritsugu, & S. Farber (Eds.), *Preventative Psychology: Theory, Research, and Practice* (pp. 199–215). New York: Pergamon Press, 1983.

Felner, R., Primavera, J., & Couce, A. The impact of school transitions: A focus for preventive efforts. *American Journal of Community Psychology,* 1981, *9,* 449–459.

Fleischman, M. J. A replication of Patterson's "Interventions for boys with conduct problems." *Journal of Consulting and Clinical Psychology,* 1981, *50,* 66–71.

Forehand, R., & Long, N. Prevention of aggression and other behavior problems in the early adolescent years. In D. Pepler & K. H. Rubin (Eds.), *The development and treatment of childhood aggression* (pp. 317–330). Hillsdale, NJ: Lawrence Earlbaum Associates, 1991.

Forgatch, M. S. The clinical science vortex: A developing theory of antisocial behavior. In D. Pepler & K. H. Rubin (Eds.), *The development and treatment of childhood aggression* (pp. 291–315). Hillsdale, NJ: Lawrence Erlbaum Associates, 1991.

Forgatch, M. S., & Patterson, G. R. *Parents and adolescents living together,* Part 2: *Family problem solving.* Eugene, OR: Castalia Publishing Company, 1989.

Forgatch, M. S., & Toobert, D. J. A cost-effective parent training program for use with normal preschool children. *Journal of Pediatric Psychology,* 1979, *4,* 129–145.

Gaffney, L. R., & McFall, R. M. A comparison of social skills in delinquent and nondelinquent adolescent girls using a behavioral role-playing inventory. *Journal of Consulting and Clinical Psychology,* 1981, 49, 959–967.

Galaway, B., Magiajlic, D., Hudson, J., Harmon, P., & McLagan, J. *International perspectives on specialist family foster care.* USA: Human Services Associates, 1990.

Gardner, F. E. Inconsistent parenting: Is there evidence for a link with children's conduct problems? *Journal of Abnormal Child Psychology,* 1988, *17,* 223–233.

Gelfand, D. M., & Teti, D. M. The effects of maternal depression on children. *Clinical Psychology Review,* 1990, *10,* 329–353.

Gleuck, S., & Gleuck, E. *Delinquents and nondelinquents in perspective.* Cambridge, MA: Harvard University Press, 1968.

Hartup, W. W. Symmetrics and asymmetries in children's relationships. In J. DeWit & H. L. Benton (Eds.), *Perspectives in child study*. Lisse, Netherlands: Zwets & Zeitlinger, 1982.

Hawkins, R. P., Almeida, M. C., Fabry, B., & Reitz, A. L. A scale to measure restrictiveness of living environments for troubled children and youths. *Hospital and Community Psychiatry*, 1992, *43*(1), 54–58.

Hawkins, R. P., Almeida, M. C., & Samet, M. *Comparative evaluation of foster family–based treatment and five other placement choices: A preliminary report*. Paper presented at the conference on Children's Mental Health Services & Policy: Building a Research Base. Tampa, Florida, February 1989.

Hawkins, R. P., & Breiling, J. (Eds.). *Therapeutic foster care: Critical issues*. Washington, DC: Child Welfare League of America, 1989.

Hawkins, R. P., Meadowcroft, P., Trout, B. A., & Luster, W. C. Foster family–based treatment. *Journal of Clinical Child Psychology*, 1985, *14*(3), 220–228.

Hazel, N. *Fostering teenagers: Two innovative schemes in Kent*. London: National Foster Care Association, 1990.

Herbert, E. W., Pinkston, E. M., Hayden, M. L., Sajwaj, T. E., Pinkston, S., Cordua, G., & Jackson, C. Adverse effects of differential parental attention. *Journal of Applied Behavior Analysis*, 1973, *6*, 15–30.

Hetherington, E. M., & Martin, B. Family interaction. In H. C. Quay & J. S. Werry (Eds.), *Psychopathological disorders of childhood* (2nd ed., pp. 247–302). New York: John Wiley & Sons, 1979.

Horner, B., Smith, V., & Ray, J. Implementing a specialized foster care project: Problems, changes, and recommendations. *Community Alternatives: International Journal of Family Care*, 1990, *2*(1), 55–76.

Hudson, J., Nutter, R., & Galaway, B. *Specialized foster family–based care: North American developments in international perspectives on specialized family foster care*. USA: Human Services Associates, 1990.

Hunt, A., Day, D. M., & Levene, K. *The parent daily report: A manual*. Toronto: Earlscourt Child & Family Centre, 1991.

Jones, R. R. "Observation" by telephone: An economical behavior sampling technique. *Oregon Research Institute Technical Report*, 1974, *4*(1).

Kazdin, A. E. *Treatment of antisocial behavior in children and adolescents*. Homewood, IL: Dorsey, 1985.

Kellam, S. G. Developmental epidemiological framework for family research on depression and aggression. In G. R. Patterson (Ed.), *Depression and aggression in family interaction* (pp. 11–48). Hillsdale, NJ: Lawrence Erlbaum Associates, 1990.

Klein, M. W. Gang cohesiveness, delinquency, and a street work program. *Journal of Research in Crime and Delinquency*, 1969, *6*, 135–166.

Klein, M. W. *Street gangs and street workers*. Englewood Cliffs, NJ: Prentice-Hall, 1971.

Kochanska, G. Affective factors in mothers' autonomy-granting to their five-year-olds: Comparison of well and depressed mothers. In T. Dix (Chair), *Emotion and parenting: The heart of the matter*. Symposium conducted at the meeting of the Society for Research in Child Development, Seattle, Washington, April 1991.

Laub, J. H., & Sampson, R. J. Unraveling families and delinquency: A reanalysis of the Gluecks' data. *Criminology*, 1988, *26*, 355–380.

Lewinsohn, P. M., & Rosenbaum, M. Recall of parental behavior by acute depressives, remitted depressives, and nondepressives. *Journal of Personality and Social Psychology*, 1987, *52*(3), 611–619.

Loeber, R., & Dishion, T. Early predictors of male delinquency: A review. *Psychological Bulletin*, 1983, *94*, 68–99.

Marcus, L. M. *Studies of attention in children vulnerable to psychopathology*. Unpublished doctoral dissertation, University of Minnesota, 1972.

Martin, C. A., & Hawkins, R. P. The restrictiveness of living environments scale: West Virginia replication of a simple device for program evaluation, policy planning, and placement decisionmaking. *Community Alternatives: International Journal of Family Care*, 1992, *4*(1), 71–79.

McCord, J. A. Some child-rearing antecedents of criminal behavior in adult men. *Journal of Personality and Social Psychology*, 1979, *9*, 1477–1486.

McCord, W., McCord, J. A., & Zola, J. K. *Origins of crime*. New York: Columbia University Press, 1959.

Miller, G. E., & Prinz, R. J. Enhancement of social learning family interventions for childhood conduct disorder. *Psychological Bulletin*, 1990, *108*(2), 291–307.

Miller, W. B. The inpact of a "total community" delinquency control project. *Social Problems*, 1962, *10*, 168–191.

Moore, K. J., & Chamberlain, P. Treatment Foster Care: Towards development of community-based models for adolescents with severe emotional and behavioral disorders. *Journal of Emotional and Behavioral Disorders*, 1994, *2*(1), 22–30.

Moore, K. J., Osgood, D. W., Larzelere, R. E., & Chamberlain, P. Pooled time–series: Its use in the evaluation of naturally occurring clinical events on problem behavior in a foster care setting. *Journal of Consulting and Clinical Psychology*, in press.

Parke, R. D. Effectiveness of punishment as an interaction of intensity, timing, agent, nurturance, and cognitive structure. *Child Development*, 1969, *40*, 213–235.

Pastorelli, C. M. *A reproduction of the Oregon Social Learning Center child treatment model*. Unpublished report. Rome: Italy, 1992.

Patterson, G. R. Reprogramming the families of aggressive boys. In C. E. Thoreson (Ed.), *Behavior modification in education*. Chicago: National Society for the Study of Education (distributed by the University of Chicago Press), 1973.

Patterson, G. R. Interventions for boys with conduct problems: Multiple settings, treatments, and criteria. *Journal of Consulting and Clinical Psychology,* 1974, *42,* 471–481.

Patterson, G. R. *Families: Applications of social learning to family life* (revised ed.). Champaign, IL: Research Press, 1975.

Patterson, G. R. The aggressive child: Victim and architect of a coercive system. In E. J. Mash, L. A. Hamerlynck, & L. C. Handy (Eds.), *Behavior modification and families:* Vol. 1, *Theory and research* (pp. 267–316). New York: Brunner/Mazel, 1976a.

Patterson, G. R. Parents and teachers as change agents: A social learning approach. In D. Olson (Ed.), *Treating relationships* (pp. 189–215). Lake Mills, IA: Graphic Press, 1976b.

Patterson, G. R. *A social interactional approach:* Vol. 3: *Coercive family process.* Eugene, OR: Castalia Publishing Company, 1982.

Patterson, G. R. Beyond technology: The next stage in developing an empirical base for parent training. In L. L'Abate (Ed.), *Handbook of family psychology and therapy* (Vol. 2, pp. 1344–1379). Homewood, IL: Dorsey, 1985.

Patterson, G. R. Performance models for antisocial boys. *American Psychologist,* 1986, *41,* 432–444.

Patterson, G. R., & Capaldi, D. M. Antisocial parents: Unskilled and vulnerable. In P. A. Cowan & E. M. Hetherington (Eds.), *Advances in family research,* II: *Family transitions* (pp. 195–218). Hillsdale, NJ: Lawrence Erlbaum Associates, 1991.

Patterson, G. R., Capaldi, D., & Bank, L. An early starter model for predicting delinquency. In D. Pepler & K. H. Rubin (Eds.), *The development and treatment of childhood aggression* (pp. 139–168). Hillsdale, NJ: Lawrence Erlbaum Associates, 1990.

Patterson, G. R., Chamberlain, P., & Reid, J. B. A comparative evaluation of a parent-training program. *Behavior Therapy,* 1982, *13,* 638–650.

Patterson, G. R., Cobb, J. A., & Ray, R. S. Direct intervention in the classroom: A set of procedures for the aggressive child. In F. W. Clark, D. R. Evans, & L. A. Hamerlynck (Eds.), *Implementing behavioral programs for schools and clinics* (pp. 151–201). Champaign, IL: Research Press, 1972.

Patterson, G. R., Dishion, T. J., & Chamberlain, P. Outcomes and methodological issues relating to treatment of antisocial children. In T. R. Giles (Ed.), *Effective psychotherapy: A handbook of comparative research.* New York: Plenum, 1993.

Patterson, G. R., & Forgatch, M. S. Therapist behavior as a determinant for client noncompliance: A paradox for the behavior modifier. *Journal of Consulting and Clinical Psychology,* 1985, *53*(6), 846–851.

Patterson, G. R., & Forgatch, M. S. *Parents and adolescents living together,* Part 1: *The basics.* Eugene, OR: Castalia Publishing Company, 1987.

Patterson, G. R., & Reid, J. B. Intervention for families of aggressive boys: A replication study. *Behavior Research and Therapy,* 1973, *11,* 383–394.

Patterson, G. R., Reid, J. B., & Dishion, T. J. *A social interactional approach,* Vol. 4: *Antisocial boys.* Eugene, OR: Castalia Publishing Company, 1992.

Patterson, G. R., Reid, J. B., Jones, R. R., & Conger, R. *A social learning approach to family intervention,* Vol. 1: *Families with aggressive children.* Eugene, Oregon: Castalia Publishing Company, 1975.

Pianta, R. C. Life stress and parenting outcomes in a disadvantaged sample: Results of the mother–child interaction project. *Journal of Child Clinical Psychology,* 1990, *19*(4), 329–337.

Pulkkinen, L. Finland: Search for alternatives to aggression. In A. P. Goldstein & M. Segall (Eds.), *Aggression in global perspective* (pp. 104–144). New York: Pergamon, 1983.

Ramscy, E., & Walker, H. M. Family management correlates of antisocial behavior among middle-school boys. *Behavioral Disorders,* 1988, *13,* 187–201.

Reid, J. B. (Ed.) *A social learning approach to family intervention,* Vol. 2: *Observation in home settings.* Eugene, OR: Castalia Publishing Company, 1978.

Reid, J. B., Hinojosa-Rivero, G., & Lorber, R. *Social learning approach to the outpatient treatment of children who steal.* Eugene, OR: Oregon Social Learning Center, unpublished manuscript, 1978.

Reid, J. B., Kavanagh, K., & Baldwin, D. Abusive parents' perceptions of child problem behaviors: An example of parental ideas. *Journal of Abnormal Child Psychology,* 1987, *15,* 457–466.

Reid, J. B., & Patterson, G. R. The modification of aggression and stealing behavior of boys in the home setting. In E. Ribes-Inesta & A. Bandura (Eds.), *Behavior modification: Experimental analysis of aggression and delinquency* (pp. 123–145). Hillsdale, NJ: Lawrence Earlbaum Associates, 1976.

Robins, L. N. *Deviant children grown up: A sociological and psychiatric study of sociopathic personality.* Baltimore, MD: Williams & Wilkins, 1966.

Robins, L. N., & Ratcliff, K. S. Risk factors in the continuation of childhood antisocial behavior into adulthood. *International Journal of Mental Health,* 1978–79, *7*(3–4), 96–116.

Roff, M. A two-factor approach to juvenile delinquency and the later histories of juvenile delinquency. In M. Roff, L. N. Robins, & M. Pollack (Eds.), *Life history research in psychopathy.* (Vol. 2, pp. 77–101). Minneapolis: University of Minnesota Press, 1972.

Rutter, M., & Quinton, D. Long-term follow-up of women institutionalized in childhood: Factors promoting good functioning in adult life. *British Journal of Developmental Psychology,* 1984, *2,* 191–204.

Rutter, M., Shaffer, D., & Sturge, C. *A guide to a multi-axial classification scheme for psychiatric disorders in childhood and adolescence.* London: University of London, 1975.

Sampson, R. J., & Laub, J. H. Crime and deviance over the life course: The salience of adult social bonds. *American Sociological Review*, 1990, *55*, 609–627.

Sawin, D. G., & Parke, R. D. Inconsistent discipline of aggression in young boys. *Journal of Experimental Child Psychology*, 1979, *28*, 525–538.

Schelle, J. A brief report on invalidity of parent evaluations of behavior change. *Journal of Applied Behavior Analysis*, 1974, *7*, 341–343.

Schur, E. M. Radical nonintervention. Englewood Cliffs, NJ: Prentice–Hall, 1973.

Sears, R. R., Maccoby, E. E., & Levin, H. *Patterns of child rearing*. Evanston, IL: Row & Peterson, 1957.

Shaffer, D., Gould, M. S., Brasic, J., Ambrosini, P., Fisher, P., Bird, H., & Aluwahlia, S. A Children's Global Assessment Scale (CGAS). *Archives of General Psychiatry*, 1983, *40*, 1228–1231.

Snyder, J. J. A reinforcement analysis of interaction in problem and nonproblem families. *Journal of Abnormal Psychology*, 1977, *86*, 528–535.

Snyder, J., & Patterson, G. R. The effects of consequences on patterns of social interaction: A quasi-experimental approach to reinforcement in natural interaction. *Child Development*, 1986, *57*, 1257–1268.

Stevens-Long, J. The effect of behavioral context on some aspects of adult disciplinary practice and affect. *Child Development*, 1973, *44*, 476–484.

Taplin, P. S., & Reid, J. B. Changes in parent consequation as a function of family intervention. *Journal of Consulting and Clinical Psychology*, 1977, *4*, 973–981.

Wahler, R. G., & Dumas, J. E. Maintenance factors in coercive mother-child interactions: The compliance and predictability hypotheses. *Journal of Applied Behavior Analysis*, 1986, *13*, 207–219.

Wahler, R. G., & Sansbury, L. E. The monitoring skills of troubled mothers: Their problems in defining child deviance. *Journal of Abnormal Child Psychology*, 1990, *18*(5), 577–589.

Walker, H. M, & Close, D. W. *Leadership training in preventing and remediating conduct disorders and antisocial behavior patterns: An interdisciplinary approach*. Eugene, OR: Center on Human Development, University of Oregon, 1992.

Walters, H. I., & Gilmore, S. K. Placebo versus social learning effect in parent training procedures designed to alter the behavior of aggressive boys. *Behavior Research and Therapy*, 1973, *4*, 361–367.

Webster-Stratton, C., & Hammond, M. Predictors of treatment outcome in parent training for families with conduct problem children. *Behavior Therapy*, 1990, *21*, 319–337.

Webster-Stratton, C., Kolpacoff, M., & Hollingsworth, T. Self-administered videotape therapy for families with conduct problem children: Comparison with two cost-effective treatments and a control group. *Journal of Consulting and Clinical Psychology*, 1988, *56*, 558–566.

Weinberg, W., & Rehmet, A. Childhood affective disorder and school problems. In D. P. Cantwell & G. A. Carlson (Eds.), *Affective disorders in childhood and adolescence: An update* (pp. 109–128). Lancaster, England: MTP Press Ltd., 1983.

Weinrott, M. R., Bauske, B., & Patterson, G. R. Systematic replication of a social learning approach. In P. O. Sjoden, S. Bates. & W. S. Dockens III (Eds.), *Trends in behavior therapy* (pp. 331–352). New York: Academic Press, 1979.

Weithorn, L. A. Mental hospitalization of troublesome youth: An analysis of skyrocketing admission rates. *Stanford Law Review,* 1988, *40,* 773–838.

Welsh, R. S. Severe parental punishment and delinquency: A developmental theory. *Journal of Clinical Child Psychology,* 1976, *5,* 17–21.

West, D. J., & Farrington, D. T. *Who becomes delinquent?* London: Heinemann Educational Books Ltd., 1973.

White, G. D., Nielsen, G., & Johnson, S. M. Time out duration and the suppression of deviant behavior in children. *Journal of Applied Behavior Analysis,* 1972, *5,* 111–120.

Wilson, H. Parental supervision re-examined. *British Journal of Criminology,* 1987, *27*(3), 215–301.

Wilson, J. Q., & Herrnstein, R. J. *Crime and human nature.* New York: Simon & Schuster, 1985.

Yost, D. M., Hochstadt, N. J., & Charles, P. Medical foster care: Achieving permanency for seriously ill children. *Children Today,* 1988, *17*(5), 22–26.

Zucker, R. A. Parental influences on the drinking patterns of their children. In M. Greenblatt & M. A. Schuckit (Eds.), *Alcoholism problems in women and children* (pp. 211–238). New York: Grune & Stratton, 1976.

Author Index

A
Ageton, S. S., 3, 11, 14
Aldridge, M. J., 18
Almeida, M. C., 1
Antoine, K., 81

B
Baldwin, D., 103
Bank, L., 3, 12, 13, 14
Bauske, B., 98
Becker, W. C., 33
Beljaars, I. C. M., 82
Bem, D. J., 14
Bereika, G. M., 95
Berger, M. A., 82
Berger, R. J., 11
Boruch, R. F., 1, 97
Boszormenyi-Nagy, I., 30
Breiling, J., 1, 95
Bryant, B., 1, 95

C
Capaldi, D. M., 6, 12, 13, 79
Caspi, A., 2, 14
Cautley, P. W., 18
Chamberlain, P., 4, 5, 11, 14, 23, 29, 46, 47, 48, 49, 51, 79, 81, 85, 90, 91, 92, 94, 95, 98, 100, 102
Charles, P., 2
Chesney-Lind, M., 11
Clement, P. W., 98
Close, D. W., 13
Cobb, J. A., 98
Coddington, R., 79
Coie, J. D., 13
Couce, A., 79

D
Day, D. M., 91
Dennis, K. W., 1, 84
Derogatis, L. R., 90
Dishion, T., 4, 11, 13, 47, 49, 98
Dodge, K. A., 92
Downey, G., 2
Dumas, J. E., 5

E
Egeland, B., 81
Elder, G. H., 2, 14
Elliott, D. S., 3, 14

F
Farber, S., 79
Farrington, D., 5, 14
Feldman, E. L., 92
Felner, R., 79
Fleischman, M. J., 100
Forehand, R., 4
Forgatch, M. S., 46, 47, 51, 53, 100

G
Gaffney, L. R., 92
Galaway, B., 1
Gardner, F. E., 5
Gelfand, D. M., 5
Gilmore, S. K., 49, 98
Gleuck, E., 5, 11
Gleuck, S., 5, 11

H
Hammond, M., 4
Hartup, W. W., 11
Hawkins, R. P., 1, 95
Hazel, N., 18, 24

Herbert, E. W., 29
Herrnstein, R. J., 11
Hetherington, E. M., 5
Hinojosa-Rivero, G., 100
Hochstadt, N. J., 2
Hollingsworth, T., 5
Horner, B., 69
Hudson, J., 1
Huizinga, D., 3, 14
Hunt, A., 91

J
Johnson, S. M., 29
Jones, R. R., 98

K
Kavanagh, K., 103
Kazdin, A. E., 5
Kellam, S. G., 6
Klein, M. W., 14
Kochanska, G., 5
Kolpacoff, M., 5
Kupersmidt, J. B., 13

L
Laub, J. H., 4, 5, 14, 47
Levene, K., 91
Levin, H., 5
Lewinsohn, P. M., 98
Loeber, R., 4
Long, N., 4

M
Maccoby, E. E., 5
Marcus, L. M., 29
Martin, B., 5
Martin, C. A., 1
McClaskey, C. L., 92
McCord, J. A., 4, 5, 47
McCord, W., 5
McFall, R. M., 92

Miller, G. E., 5
Miller, W. B., 14
Milne, P. C., 98
Moore, K. J., 19, 79

N
Nielsen, G., 29
Nutter, R., 1

P
Parke, R. D., 5, 33
Pastorelli, C. M., 91
Patterson, G. R., 3, 4, 5, 6, 11, 12, 13, 29, 30, 45, 47, 49, 51, 53, 55, 79, 90, 98, 100
Pianta, R. C., 81
Primavera, J., 79
Prinz, R. J., 5
Pulkkinen, L., 5

Q
Quinton, D., 5

R
Ramsey, E., 13
Ratcliff, K. S., 14
Ray, J., 14, 49, 69
Ray, R. S., 98
Rehmet, A., 6
Reid, J. B., 3, 4, 5, 11, 13, 23, 46, 51, 85, 90, 91, 92, 94, 95, 98, 100, 102, 103
Robins, L. N., 2, 14
Roff, M., 11
Rosenbaum, M., 98
Rutter, M., 5

S
Samet, M., 1
Sampson, R. J., 4, 6, 14, 47
Sansbury, L. E., 5
Sawin, D. G., 5
Schelle, J., 98

Schur, E. M., 11
Sears, R. R., 5
Shaffer, D., 5, 90
Smith, V., 69
Snyder, J. J., 13
Spencer, P. M., 90
Stevens-Long, J., 5
Sturge, C., 5

T

Taplin, P. S., 5
Teti, D. M., 5
Toobert, D. J., 100

W

Wahler, R. G., 5
Walker, H. M., 13
Walters, H. I., 49, 98

Webster-Stratton, C., 4, 5
Weinberg, W., 6
Weinrott, M. R., 98
Weithorn, L. A., 19
Welsh, R. S., 11
West, D. J., 14
White, G. D., 29
Wilson, H., 5
Wilson, J. Q., 11
Wothke, W., 97

Y

Yost, D. M., 2

Z

Zola, J. K., 5
Zucker, R. A., 5